Trotsky

Trotsky

David Renton

HAUS PUBLISHING • LONDON

First published in Great Britain in 2004 by
Haus Publishing Limited
26 Cadogan Court, Draycott Avenue
London SW3 3BX

Copyright © 2004

The moral right of the authors has been asserted

A CIP catalogue record for this book is available from the British Library

ISBN 1-904341-62-4

Designed and typeset in Garamond
Printed and bound by Graphicom in Vicenza, Italy

Front cover: photograph of Leon Trotsky courtesy of Topham Picture Point
Back cover: photograph courtesy of AKG-Images

CONDITIONS OF SALE
All rights reserved. No part of this publication may be reproduced, stored in a
retrieval system, or transmitted in any form or by any means, electronic,
mechanical, photocopying, recording or otherwise, without the prior permission
of the publisher

This book is sold subject to the condition that it shall not, by way of trade
or otherwise, be lent, re-sold, hired out or otherwise circulated without
the publisher's prior consent in any form of binding or cover other than
that in which it is published and without a similar condition including
this condition being imposed on the subsequent purchaser

Contents

Introduction

Some historical figures have long remained a puzzle to historians. George Orwell's biographers have yet to decide whether he was really an anarchist or a Tory. Rosa Luxemburg has been remembered both for her life and for the events of her death, for her love letters and for her radical pamphlets. William Shakespeare, Roger Casement, Albert Einstein – each generation has painted them anew. With Leon Trotsky, however, the biographer's task is much simpler. The friendliest and the most hostile of historians unite in representing Trotsky as the 'eternal revolutionary' (in the words of Dimitri Volkogonov) or the 'rebel *par excellence*' (Isaac Deutscher), a Prometheus or Mephistopheles, the very incarnation of the spirit of revolt.[1]

Any contradictions in Trotsky's personality did not originate with him, but lay rather in the nature of the Russian Revolution itself; for any successful uprising must combine upheaval in the state with moments of restoration afterwards. Trotsky's critics allege that his lifelong preoccupation with the cause of the underdog faded after 1917, when he and his allies took power. Had not Trotsky resorted to terror when faced with the onslaught of civil war? Deutscher's 'rebel *par excellence*' was meant ironically, to highlight the awkward corner in which Trotsky found himself after 1921, when he argued that the techniques of compulsion that had won the civil war should now be employed by a civilian army in a time of peace. This episode is discussed more fully below.

A different charge was also sometimes laid against Trotsky in his pomp. He was said to be proud or overbearing and far too aware of his talents. One colleague, the Bolshevik playwright and commissar Anatoly Lunacharsky referred to Trotsky's 'colossal arrogance and

[his] inability or unwillingness to show any human kindness or to be attentive to people'. Yet Lunacharsky was also aware of Trotsky's better qualities, including his sure choice of revolutionary tactics and his skills as a speaker and writer. Lunacharsky could at least admit that Trotsky and Lenin are 'two of the strongest of the strong'.[2]

Trotsky's self-confidence combined the cheek of a middleclass boy who had broken all links to his class with the arrogance of a skilled rhetorician with an adoring audience. He was also a brilliant and original theorist whose most famous predictions were borne out by events. He was the man who led the second Russian Revolution, who founded the Red Army and who along with Lenin did more than anyone else to found the Soviet state. He was also the first and most sustained and determined critic of that society when it emerged. Trotsky was the man who refused to compromise, who followed the Revolution to its end, who wrote and argued and never gave up. Other Communists who lost faith in the society they had built kept their doubts to themselves, but of all the leading Bolsheviks who rejected Stalin, Trotsky was the only one who fought back. He even gave his life in that struggle.

From Hope to Revolt (1879–1898)

Leon Trotsky's real name was Lev Davidovich Bronstein and he was born in southern Russia on 26 October 1879. Both 'Lev' and 'Leon' translate as 'lion' – 'Trotsky' was a much later pseudonym. His grandfather, Leon Bronstein, had left the small Jewish town near Poltava where he had grown up to seek a new life in the countryside around Kherzon. Trotsky's father, David Bronstein, was the only one of several children who made a successful living on the land. He became a prosperous farmer, owning 250 acres in his own name and holding another 400 on lease. He was a rare creature indeed in nineteenth-century Russia, for only in the southern plains of the Tsar's empire were Jewish families even allowed to possess their own land, while many Jews had strong cultural prejudices against farming. The peasant lifestyle was seen as vulgar and incompatible with a study of scripture, the only proper calling for an educated Jew.

In the 1870s David Bronstein bought a farm in the village of Yanokva, near the town of Bobrinets in the Kirovograd region of the Ukraine. He was illiterate, but skilled with his hands. Through patient accumulation he became rich enough to own his own hut with five rooms, wooden floors and a straw roof. *My childhood was not one of hunger and cold* Trotsky later recalled. *My family had already achieved a competence at the time of my birth. But it was the stern competence of people still rising from poverty and having no desire to stop halfway. Every muscle was strained, every thought set on work and savings.* Trotsky never romanticized his childhood: *Life strikes the weak – and who is weaker than a child?*[3]

In his biography of the young Lenin, written in the 1930s, Trotsky insisted that the future leader of the Revolution had only slowly learned political consciousness. *Vladimir retained his*

religious faith up to the age of sixteen . . . There is not a single instance on record, either in school or outside of it, of [Lenin] *evoking by word or deed any adverse opinion from the authorities and teachers of his school.*[4] Trotsky's point was then to rescue his friend from the wild praise of too many sycophants. Yet the parallels with his own life are equally important. Even the most single-minded revolutionary must have a childhood. His early memories were of his parents' farm. *I must have been about four years old when someone put me on the back of a big grey mare as gentle as a sheep, with neither bridle nor saddle, only a rope halter. I spread my legs wide apart and held on to the mane with both hands. The mare quietly took me to a pear tree and walked under a branch, which caught me across the middle. Not realizing what the matter was, I slid over the mare's rump and hit the grass. I was not hurt, only puzzled.*[5] Later he was sent to fetch eggs from the gap under the barn. The farm was a world of dogs, storks, cows, pigs and chickens. The sheds held wheat, barley, winter rape and oats. The barns and outhouses were built from mud and twigs.

He was the fifth child in his family. One brother and two sisters would eventually survive into adulthood and they were his guides on the farm. They also gave him his first books to read. Trotsky was not good at sports such as swimming or skating, but he made up for this with a keen sense of irony, using jokes to win friends. One ally was Gryeben, the farm mechanic, whom the young

Trotsky would help by turning wheels or working the bellows in his shed. Sometimes he was even allowed to cut the threads of screws in the machine shop. Trotsky enjoyed this work and liked to see the results of his efforts in his hands. (He also admired Constantine, the miller who dallied with Katy the cook, though he was sorry they could not afford the ten roubles it cost to get married.) There were other outlets for Trotsky's creativity. A cousin taught him to draw caricatures and they produced a magazine. He also wrote poems, which his father asked him to read to their guests.

Aged seven, Trotsky was sent to school where he studied Russian, mathematics and Hebrew. He recalled little of this time, except for the slate blackboard and the teacher's pen. Most pupils spoke Yiddish, but Trotsky's family spoke Russian. At this time he stayed with his Uncle Abram and Aunt Rachel, who were rather aloof. Happily his former nurse, Masha, was now a servant in Abram's house. Masha had several admirers and when she eventually fell pregnant Rachel scolded her for her immorality. Trotsky watched as the illegitimate child was born.

He was still attached to a domestic world of stoves, yards and kitchens. One Christmas, he was enchanted by a troop of actors, led by a worker named Prokhor. Trotsky offered to be their scribe

Vladimir Ilyich Lenin (1870–1924) was born in Simbirsk to a family of provincial bureaucrats. His political awakening came in May 1887 when his brother was executed for conspiring to kill Alexander III. Lenin drew two lasting lessons from this affair: (1) a permanent hostility towards Russia's rulers, and (2) an equally obdurate rejection of the tactics employed by his brother. Lenin was expelled from Kazan University for participating in student protests. In 1903 he was instrumental in causing the split between the Bolsheviks and the Mensheviks (the two separate groups of the RSDPL). In 1917 he played a decisive role in urging his comrades to seize power. Later he became leader of the Union of Soviet Socialist Republics (USSR).

to record Prokhor's speeches for posterity, but his father dragged him away before he could embarrass his parents.

One summer Trotsky's cousin Moissey Filippovich Schpentzer came visiting from Odessa. He had suffered from tuberculosis and needed fresh country air to recover. Schpentzer was 28, witty and charming and he filled young Trotsky's mind with new ideas. He had been a student, but had been thrown out of the university for a political offence. He then worked as a journalist and as a statistician. Now he was translating Greek tragedies and publishing short stories for children and was poised to marry a school principal.

Schpentzer's energetic presence dominated the household and there were few peaceful moments. Trotsky vividly remembered how, seeing a foreman strike a peasant, Schpentzer had hissed 'How shameful!' Schpentzer cultivated his clever young cousin, teaching him grammar and mathematics and buying him a stack of books. Diligently and with growing confidence, Trotsky worked his way through this treasure trove. Schpentzer had brought the thrill of city life to Trotsky's boyhood and it proved infectious.

David Bronstein engaged his son in keeping the farm accounts. In the early 1920s the American journalist Max Eastman (1883–1969) interviewed Trotsky on several occasions to build up a picture of his childhood. He describes Bronstein's 'imperious secretary' at the age of eight or nine: 'Sitting there with his big blank books, a big inkwell and pen, a big shock of darkening hair, but everything else about him incredibly small, his legs reaching only halfway down to the floor, he had nevertheless a very important, rapid and solemnly competent manner of doing what had to be done, changing and dealing out money, noting down the amounts paid and the amounts received.'[6]

There were further hints of the life ahead: 'One day a neighbour's horse broke into his father's wheatfield. The neighbour's horses were always breaking into his father's fields. His father had so many fields. And perhaps it wasn't just the horses who were so clever. At any rate his father was very severe in the administration of justice on these occasions. He locked the horse up and told the peasant he would let him out when the damages were paid. Trotsky saw his father striding back into the house and the poor peasant coming after him with his hat in his hand, crying: "I didn't see him. It wasn't my fault! I didn't see him, it wasn't my fault!", bent over as though he were a little old woman who needed help. Trotsky ran into his mother's bedroom and into the bed by the window. He lay there curled up on the blanket, crying.

'It was dark and it was dinnertime, but he did not answer when they called him to dinner. He felt all the sorrow in the world then and he looked out of the window in the dark. His mother finally got up from the table to look for him, calling out of both doors and receiving no answer. She found him at last. Perhaps he let her hear a sob from the bedroom. But she came back without him. "That's a queer child," she said. "He's been crying for a half an hour and I don't know what he's crying about." His father was more understanding. "I think he heard Ivan wailing about that horse," he said. "Tell him Ivan has the horse and he didn't pay anything." So Trotsky found himself in the embarrassing position of having to stop crying suddenly because he had made a mistake. He managed it by denying that he had been crying about Ivan's horse, and coming up to the table snuffling and pouting in a solemn way, as though he had been communing with some sorrow too deep for grown-up people to understand.'[7]

Trotsky's mother, Anna, had lived in Odessa and was more cultured than her husband. She probably married for love and perhaps without her parents' blessing. She subscribed to a lending library and read to the children, for she knew the importance of a good education. Nevertheless, Trotsky was closer to his father. *When we were young, my father was quieter and gentler with us than my mother. My mother would often lose her temper with us, sometimes without reason, and would vent on us her failure or chagrin over some domestic failure. We always found it more remunerative to ask our father for favours rather than our mother.* But over time, his father became just as strict. *The cause of this lay in the hardships of his life, in the cares which grew as his business increased, and more especially in the conditions of the agrarian crisis of the Eighties, as well as in the disappointment which his children gave him.*[8]

Of all Trotsky's early alliances, the one with his cousin proved the most fruitful. Aged nine he was sent to stay with Schpentzer and his wife in Odessa, for schooling. This was the first great upheaval in Trotsky's life. Odessa was 'Russia's Marseilles' and far from typical of the Russian provinces.[9] The architecture was neo classical, designed on French models. The train station connected Odessa to Moscow and Kiev. The streets were gas-lit and paved with granite. It could not have been more different from the world Trotsky had known. Odessa was a diverse and cosmopolitan port of some 300,000 people, with Greeks and Jews living side by side with Germans and Russians. It was not always a happy mix, however, and in 1871 and 1881 anti-Jewish pogroms resulted in several deaths.

Staying with his cousin, even Trotsky's domestic routine changed. He was sent to bed regularly at the same hour and taught to say 'Good morning'. He learned to keep his hands and nails clean and discovered that the language of his parents was not pure Russian, but mixed with Ukrainian. The conversation was far more refined at Schpentzer's house.

It was a rare education. Trotsky studied the classics and theatre at home and helped his cousin as he built up a publishing house. *I lived for six years with this family, during the first period of the publishing concern. I became familiar with type, make-up, layout, printing, paging and binding. Proofreading was my favourite pastime.*[10]

He was sent to a school established by the Lutheran parish to serve Odessa's German population, but in Trotsky's day the

Germans were being slowly forced out. They made up around half of the student body when he began, but much less in his final years. Although he remained poor at games, he was a successful scholar and thrived in that competitive atmosphere. All homework was graded from one to five and everyone in his class soon knew of the top marks that their fellow pupil had scored. Friends from this period remembered him as a diligent, neat and organized young man, as well as being polite and well-dressed – rare virtues in an adolescent boy. For all his triumphs, however, two clashes with the school authorities hinted at Trotsky's future direction.

The first occurred in his second year. One of the boys, Vakker, was behind with his work. He had failed the year once and if he failed a second time he would be sent home. So when a teacher named Burnande announced that Vakker had scored such a low mark that he would be excluded, Vakker spent the rest of the day crying. Trotsky immediately organized a protest, loosely modelled on a concert to which his uncle had taken him. When Burnande turned his back to leave the room, his exit was welcomed with a chorus of boos from the entire class. The teacher turned to face the class: silence. He turned back: more booing. Accused of hatching a plot, the terrified Vakker identified Trotsky as the culprit and he was expelled for the rest of the school year. Much to Trotsky's surprise, his parents loved to hear the story of how he had been expelled. Instead of reprimanding him, they made him repeat the story to their friends, much to his embarrassment.

The next few years of Trotsky's life passed without incident. He went back to school and continued to do well in his studies. His father organized a class in the holidays so that his son could learn to read the Bible in Hebrew. It soon turned out that the elderly bearded teacher was an atheist, as was the young Trotsky.

At 16 Trotsky was involved in a second protest. The teacher of Russian was so lazy that he could not even bother to mark their essays. One morning, having announced yet again that he would return their papers tomorrow and that in the meantime the class should prepare a new composition, he was surprised to hear one of the students declare: 'I won't write a new essay until you've marked my last one.' Trotsky leapt to the boy's defence: *He is entirely right. You should correct our first papers before you ask us to write a second!*[11] The complaining boy was expelled and Trotsky was punished with a long period of solitary detention.

Trotsky chose to complete his studies in Nikolaev, a medium-sized town close to his parents' home. He found lodgings and dressed in a European fashion during these months. He had his hair cropped and wore an expensive tan suit and a new hat. His visits home were difficult. Although his parents were immensely proud of their elegant, educated son, it seemed odd to them that he had learned so little about farming. Trotsky describes watching his father threshing grain with a purposeful balanced rhythm that the proud adolescent could not hope to match. Bronstein hoped his son might go to university and train as an engineer, yet the idea held no attraction for Trotsky. They fought furiously, but despite Trotsky's stubbornness, he had no firm beliefs other than a conviction that he should be master of his own fate.

Trotsky was a rebel without a cause. The 16 year old had yet to work out his politics. Ideas were accumulated, but slowly. In Nikolaev he met a bookseller named Galatsky who provided him with a stock of banned populist tracts and novels. Later, an old schoolfriend invited him to join a discussion circle hosted by Franz Franzevich Shvigovsky, a Czech radical who made a living selling fruit and vegetables from his garden. The group was composed of students and workers who were able to speak freely in Shvigovsky's orchard garden. Police spies infiltrated the group, but quickly dismissed them as a bunch of idle dreamers.

So who was Lev Davidovich Bronstein before he became Leon Trotsky? A tall, self-confident young man, he had an aptitude for languages and creative writing. He had read widely, but superficially. He expressed himself confidently in generalities, but lacked an adult's memory for detail. He was introspective and afraid of rejection. He struck poses and could talk himself into believing anything. In particular, he was cynical about any collective or mass movement. He was lonely and kept his desires hidden. He was in turns disagreeable, likeable and ridiculous. His family was prosperous but common, whereas he aspired to be cultured, though he did not fear poverty. He wanted to challenge authority, but lacked a conspirator's talent for organization. He hoped to be a writer, but lacked the ability or experience to shape his material and make it his own. He was vain and conceited, yet showed promise, though his views were still those of a romantic rather than a revolutionary.

Alexander III (1845–94) became Tsar after the assassination of his father, Alexander II, and ruled Russia from 1881–94. An autocratic Tsar, he cancelled all plans for a representative assembly and pursued a repressive policy against those seeking political reform. Despite several assassination attempts, he died a natural death and was succeeded by his son, Nicholas II.

In order to understand Lev Davidovich's political conversion we need to see it in the context of the times. The radicals of the 1890s regarded Russia under Alexander III and then under his son, Nicholas II, as a prison society. At the top of the pyramid was the imperial family and a few hereditary nobles organized into a complex hierarchy of military orders. Beneath them was a larger group of merchants, wealthy peasants and a few thousand indigenous Russian capitalists. There were about a million workers, plus large numbers of urban poor. At the very bottom of the heap came the peasants – the majority of the population – some of whom could remember the time of serfdom, which had ended only in 1861. For decades young left-wing intellectuals had talked about 'going to the people'. Twice in the 1870s a whole generation of students had descended on the country in the vain hope of stirring up an insurrection against Alexander II.

Tsar Nicholas II and the Russian Royal Family; Tsarevich Alexei, Grand Duchesses
Olga, Marie, Tatiana, Anastasia and the Tsarina Alexandra 1915

Nicholas II (1868–1918), the last Tsar of Russia, ruled from 1894 to 1917. His ambitions in Asia caused the Russo-Japanese War (1904–5), which in turn led to the Revolution of 1905. He established a Duma or parliament in 1906, but it was too late for real reform. In 1915 he took supreme command of Russian forces in the First World War, leaving Russia to the mismanagement of Tsarina Alexandra (1872–1918) and her favourite Grigori Efimovich Rasputin (c.1872–1916). After the Russian Revolution of 1917, Nicholas was forced to abdicate. He and his family were imprisoned by the Bolsheviks and executed at Ekaterinburg.

Many Russian intellectuals followed the ideas of populism or 'Narodism', but their philosophy was diffuse. Narodism was chaotic, spiritualistic, moralistic and elitist – a very Russian mixture of liberalism and anarchism. Narodniks spoke of 'justice' and 'progress' and figures such as Sergei Nechaev (1847–82) insisted that a small group of revolutionaries might even be able to hold power against the Tsar. *What Is to Be Done?* (1863), the famous novel by Nikolai Chernyshevsky (1828–89), dramatizes the populist case. In March 1881 the Narodniks even succeeded in assassinating Alexander II (1818–81). The result, however, was only another period of state repression.

From the Russian word for 'the people', *'narod'*, they took the name 'Narodniks'.

The Russian villages, meanwhile, were already organized in a sort of co-operative structure under the leadership of local peasant elders. These *mir* were hardly revolutionary and in most places barely representative. Women were excluded from all debates and the owners of the largest tracts of land had the most influence. Yet these village communes were the closest that Russia came to democracy at the time. This led some intellectuals to hope that by uniting the villages the nation could be transformed into a democratic peasant society. Such 'socialism' would absolve Russia from the necessity of going through a capitalist stage. In any other country the dreams of the Narodniks might have seemed romantic, diffuse, even moderate, but in a society crawling with spies they could not organize legally. They were compelled, therefore, to adopt the most extreme tactics. What was a terrorist, argued their left-wing critics, but a liberal with a gun?[12]

A serf was an unfree peasant bound to the land he worked. He paid the lord of the manor a fee and provided services in return for protection and the use of the land. While serfdom declined in Western Europe in the late Middle Ages, it was not abolished in Eastern Europe until the nineteenth century.

Philosopher and political economist Karl Marx photographed in London 1856

These were the ideas discussed in Shvigovsky's orchard: the ideals of the Russian populists and the history of their struggle. Trotsky was won over immediately. Interpreting one aspect of the Narodnik legacy as a vow of poverty, he quickly got rid of the expensive suit. Any spare money he spent on books and his appearance changed sufficiently for his landlady to wonder sadly what had gone wrong.

For all the evident appeal of the populist tradition, by the mid 1890s Narodism was being challenged by new socialist theories. The most important arguments were those associated with the German philosopher, economist and revolutionary, Karl Marx. In contrast to the Narodniks, the early Russian Marxists argued that economic laws could not be broken and Russia would inevitably have to endure some period of Western-style capitalism before any kind of socialism was possible. Support for the new socialist era would come from the workers, the majority of the future, and only a mass movement could bring about a socialist society. The founders of Russian Marxism – Georgi Plekhanov, Paul Axelrod and Vera Zasulich – firmly rejected the elitism of the Narodniks.

Plekhanov and his allies were an impressive generation of leaders. Zasulich had been a Narodnik and a successful defendant in a show trial, before converting to Marxism. For his part, Plekhanov

Born in the Rhineland, Karl Marx (1818–83) was active in the German Revolution of 1848 and played a leading role in the International Working Men's Association, the First International. In such insightful works as *The Communist Manifesto* (1848) and *Capital* (1867–85) he set out to explain modern society. Marx predicted that industrial capitalist economies would dominate the world and that a new class of people, the industrial working class, would become increasingly powerful in society. For the first time in human history, he argued, socialism and democracy could be achieved if these ideas had the support of the workers, who were rapidly becoming the majority.

Born in Tambov to an aristocratic family, Georgi Plekhanov (1856–1918) left university to dedicate himself to the Revolution. He launched the first Russian Marxist group, *the Emancipation of Labour*, in 1883 and helped to found *Iskra ('The Spark')*, the newspaper on which Lenin, Julius Martov (1873–1923) and Trotsky left their mark. After 1903 Plekhanov supported the Mensheviks against the Bolsheviks. In 1914 he backed the army, when many Russian socialists argued for peace. From then on, Plekhanov was an embarrassment to his one-time comrades. He died in Finland, an enemy of the October Revolution of 1917, which established the ruling Soviet of People's Commissars under Lenin's chairmanship.

had broken from populism in the 1870s and earned a reputation as the founder of Russian Marxism. After Plekhanov's death, Trotsky described with great admiration the crucial role he had played in establishing an indigenous Russian left wing. *This was a truly great man. And into the history of Russian social thought he has entered as a great figure. Plekhanov did not create the theory of historical materialism. He did not enrich it with new scientific achievements. But he introduced it into Russian life. And this is a merit of enormous significance. Plekhanov did not create the materialist dialectic, but he was its convinced, passionate and brilliant crusader in Russia from the beginning of the Eighties. And this required the greatest penetration, a broad historical outlook and a noble courage of thought. These qualities Plekhanov combined also with a brilliancy of exposition and an endowment of wit. The first Russian crusader for Marxism wielded the sword famously. And how many wounds he inflicted!*[13]

At the end of the 1890s a second generation of Marxists began to emerge. They, too, accepted that the whole world was entering a capitalist era that Russia could not evade. In the hands of such diligent professors as the Ukrainian economist Mikhail Tugan-Baranovsky (1865–1919) and Marxist philosopher Nikolai Berdyaev (1874–1948),[14] Marx was reshaped to become just another learned economist. He was said to have 'proved' that all countries, even Russia, would inevitably be sucked into the new capitalist world order, but these 'legal Marxists' placed less emphasis on the revolutionary defeat of capitalism. Social justice might have to wait for a while, they argued, until the economic conditions were in place, but this delay was all to the good. After all, history could not be rushed. Capitalism was at least a more advanced system than Tsarist feudalism and its ascendancy would eventually result in a long period of democratic rule. The champion of 'legal Marxism', Peter Struve (1870–1944), would eventually become leader of the right-wing Kadet Party. By 1917, indeed, not just the left but even the right and centre of Russian politics were led by former Marxists. Although Struve's apostasy belonged to the future, there were hints of it in the 1890s and we can understand, therefore, some of the caution with which young intellectuals viewed this new strain of 'Marxism'.

These grand political and philosophical ideas were not restricted to a few leaders publishing pamphlets in exile. They were discussed across Russia by students and young workers determined to overthrow the Tsar. Protests took place throughout the country and

An early correspondent with Marx, Vera Zasulich (1851–1919) shot General Trepov, the Governor of St Petersburg, in January 1878 in protest at his mistreatment of a political prisoner. Evidence came out of at her trial of repeated police abuses and she was acquitted. The police tried to seize her outside the court, but were prevented by a crowd of supporters. Zasulich escaped into exile where she followed Plekhanov from populism to Marxism. She served on the editorial board of *Iskra* and allied herself with the Mensheviks.

Marx's materialist interpretation of history (historical materialism) argues that social, cultural and political phenomena are determined by the mode of production of material things. As a result he gave priority to the economy to explain historical processes.

Trotsky was 17 when he met Alexandra Sokolovskaya (1873–1938). She was his first love and followed him to Siberia. His family disapproved of their marriage, blaming her for their son's inflammatory politics. Trotsky left Alexandra and travelled to London in 1902, although they were never legally divorced and their separation seems to have been amicable. When Trotsky, his second wife Natalia and their two sons met Alexandra and Trotsky's two daughters in post-revolutionary Russia, there was no suggestion of animosity or jealousy. Arrested on Stalin's orders in 1935, Alexandra was deported to Tobolsk in western Siberia, where she died.

Trotsky's friends engaged him in heated debates. One in particular, a student in her mid-twenties named Alexandra Sokolovskaya, had adopted Plekhanov's Marxism with its emphasis on the urban working class. Later she recalled the rumours that surrounded the young Trotsky. Having been told he was a great debater and the champion of a remorseless logic, she expected some bearded professor, so she was disappointed to find her new adversary was a mere youth of 17. Another Marxist student found him to be 'the most audacious and determined controversialist' of the group and Trotsky enjoyed denouncing Alexandra with a 'pitiless sarcasm'.[15]

During these arguments Trotsky supported the vigorous peasant socialism of the Narodniks and derided Marxism as didactic, mechanical and materialistic. Where in any of its books did one find love, spirit or anger? he asked. When did any Marxist rage against the injustices of life? His own preferred motto was the Latin phrase *dum spiro, spero*: 'while I breathe, I hope'. This angry young man enjoyed baiting Alexandra. He once wrote a letter to the public library asking it to cancel her subscription to her favourite journal, *New Life*, which had recently been won over to Marxism. It was a petty gesture that reduced her to tears. Yet for all Trotsky's bluster, Alexandra was slowly persuading him of the worth of Marxism. Like many of the young men who chatted with her in Shvigovsky's orchard, he had fallen in love.

At the end of the academic year Trotsky found himself back at home with his father, who still hoped his son might find a proper career. Their arguments grew increasingly bitter and neither man would back down. Eventually, through the intervention of an uncle, the decision was deferred: Trotsky agreed to study mathematics at Odessa University. Back in 'Russia's Marseilles', he spent the autumn doing odd jobs, teach-

Trotsky in his student years

ing at a school, arguing with the older generation. He passed round political leaflets in his uncle's factory and attended the occasional lecture at the university. But only one subject occupied his thoughts: the task of spreading socialist ideas among the people. Finally, in the winter of 1896, Trotsky slipped away from Odessa and returned to the familiar charms of Shvigovsky's orchard in Nikolaev.

Reunited with Alexandra, his antagonism to Marxism surfaced once again.[16] He teased her: *How on earth can a young girl so full of life stand that dry, narrow, impractical stuff?* 'How on earth,' she replied, 'can a person who thinks he is logical be contented with a head full of vague, idealistic emotions?'[17] On New Year's Eve Trotsky finally announced that he had been won over to Marxism. His friends were surprised, but toasts were duly drunk to the victory of the working class. When Trotsky's turn came, he

The photograph which appeared an early search warrant for Trotsky. 1895

lifted his glass and shouted: *A curse on all Marxists and upon those who want to bring dryness and harshness into all relations of life!*[18] It was another of his practical jokes, but Alexandra was not impressed. She left, vowing never to see him again.

After a few weeks she returned and the two adversaries were reconciled. They even worked together on a campaign to democratize the local library. Membership fees were to be increased, but Trotsky and Alexandra successfully overturned this decision at a public meeting.[19] Around this time he also began writing a play to show the superiority of Narodism over Marxism, but friends who read it objected that he had given the Marxist character all the best lines. The heroine's opinions were also markedly similar to Alexandra's.

For the first time in his life Trotsky had neglected his studies and his parents were concerned. On a brief return to Yanokva, his father was livid when Trotsky spoke of overthrowing the Tsar. Taking a defiant stand, Trotsky gave up his allowance and moved in with Shvigovsky in Nikolaev. His father travelled there to see him and accused Trotsky's friends of having deserted their parents, as had his own son.

In the spring of 1897 Trotsky announced that he had decided to organize the workers in Nikolaev's factories. Would his friends join him? The idea was already in the air: large unions had recently been founded in Moscow and Kiev. One of Trotsky's friends recalled that Trotsky 'suddenly called me aside and proposed in great secrecy that I join a working-men's association, organized by himself . . . The Narodnik idea, Bronstein [Trotsky] said,

The engineer and socialist Ivan Mukhin (1870–1920) was the public face of the South Russian Workers' Union. After the Revolution, Trotsky and Mukhin met again in the Ukraine. Elected to the central committee of the Ukrainian Communist Party, he died shortly afterwards in an epidemic.

had been discarded; the organization was planned to be social democratic, although Bronstein avoided using this term . . . When I joined the organization, everything had been arranged. Bronstein had already established his contacts with the workers and also with the revolutionary circles in Odessa, Ekaterinoslav and other towns.'[20] Not yet 18, Trotsky had decided to be a leader of men, but as Alexandra had the good grace not to point out, if he had decided to focus on the factory workers he must have finally discarded his peasant populism in favour of the proletarian values of Marx.

The mood of the workers was supportive and early contacts were made along friendship networks to avoid police detection. One group of workers already belonged to a Christian society and took full part in the socialist discussions. At the early meetings, a factory worker named Ivan Mukhin showed more courage in persuading his fellow workers of the socialist cause than the fresh-faced intellectuals who saw themselves as the leaders of the group. Trotsky remembered him as a thin man with a pointed beard and a shrewd, apprehensive look.

He later recalled how Mukhin had taught him to make the case for socialism using just a handful of beans. '"It's very simple," he would say. "I put a bean on the table and say, 'This is the Tsar.' Around it, I place more beans. 'These are ministers, bishops, generals and over there are the gentry and the merchants. And in this other heap, the plain people.' Now I ask, 'Where is the Tsar?' They point to the centre. 'Where are the ministers?' They point to those around. Just as I have told them, they answer. Now, wait," and at this point Mukhin completely closed his left eye and paused. "Then I scramble all the beans together," he went on. "I say, 'Now tell me where is the Tsar? The ministers?' And they answer me, 'Who can tell? You can't spot them now' . . . And so I say, 'All beans should be scrambled.'"[21]

There was enough support for these Nikolaev workers and students to call themselves the South Russian Workers' Union. The name came from a previous group formed in 1875 whose history was not auspicious. The police had arrested its leaders, one of whom, N P Schedrin, was twice condemned to death before having his sentence commuted to hard labour. For many years he was chained to a wheelbarrow. Later he was tortured in the Schüsselburg fortress and remained there for 15 years, a powerful symbol of martyrdom to the radicals of later years.[22]

Unlike its predecessor, the South Russian Workers' Union went from strength to strength. Once the group reached 25 members it split and a second branch was established. Labourers joined, as well as cabinet-makers, shipwrights, compositors and electricians. The workers of Nikolaev were well paid, literate and highly skilled and already enjoyed an eight-hour day, so they did not ask the students for advice on how to organize strikes. They wanted something more than higher wages. They wanted equality. Union membership swelled, as if people had simply been waiting for it to come into being, and some union members even dedicated marching tunes to the memory of Marx and Engels. In the end, there were eight or nine branches of the South Russian Workers' Union in a city of fewer than 10,000 workers.

Much of the success of the union was down to the boundless energy of the young Trotsky. He drew up a constitution, edited

Friedrich Engels the foremost authority on Marx and Marxism

the magazine *Our Cause* and took responsibility for all aspects of the printing process, writing text and cutting stencils. He even delivered his first public speech, a mixture of sharp debate and false oratory. Trotsky quoted the anthropologist Ludwig Gumplowitz (1838–1909) and the British economist and philosopher John Stuart Mill (1806–73), losing himself in a fog of long words and grand ideas. His audience was equally baffled. His Marxist comrades did not know how to respond and Trotsky felt terribly ashamed at his pretension. Nevertheless, the course of Trotsky's life had now been set. Where once there was irony and scorn, there was now energy and will. His life as a political activist had begun.

Trotsky and his student friends were astonished at their success. They covered Nikolaev with socialist slogans so that no citizen could ignore the Revolution. The South Russian Workers' Union soon gained a reputation for militancy and other socialist groups began to make tentative contact. As did the police, though they were

The German sociologist Friedrich Engels (1820–95) co-authored *The Communist Manifesto* with Karl Marx. He also introduced Marx to British economic conditions and the working-class movement. Among other books he wrote *The Condition of the Working Class in England in 1844* (1845) and after Marx's death he edited the last volume of *Capital* (1885).

slow to act. It was hard to believe that the agitation in the factories and on the docks had anything to do with the bohemian students in Shvigovsky's orchard. In January 1898, however, the police finally arrested 28 leaders of the union. Only six members were identified as intellectuals (including Trotsky), the rest were workers and the very worst punishments were reserved for them. Some went mad, others committed suicide.

Trotsky was kept in solitary confinement in Kherzon Prison. Interrogation was minimal and he was never informed of any charges against him. Prison life was monotonous and Trotsky was not allowed any exercise or contact with other prisoners. Even neighbouring cells were kept empty to prevent any communication. His cell was full of lice and other vermin. He had no soap, no change of clothing and no blankets in the winter. The worst torment was being denied access to books or writing materials. He composed poems in his head and passed the time by counting out 1,111 footsteps on the diagonal between the opposite corners of his room.

After what seemed like an eternity, Trotsky was transferred to a prison in Odessa. He was still in solitary confinement, but he communicated covertly with prisoners in the neighbouring cells. At last he had access to books. Despite being a confirmed atheist, he reread the Bible in German, French, Italian and English. He also consulted the polemics of the Orthodox priests against the authors of 'atheist tracts' – such as the French moralist Voltaire (1694–1778), the German philosopher Immanuel Kant (1724–1804) and the naturalist Charles Darwin (1809–1882) – hoping to find traces of the very texts that were being denounced. Two years of Trotsky's life were wasted in prison. He and Alexandra were then sentenced to four further years of internal exile in Siberia.

The Pen (1899–1903)

The prospect of exile held few terrors for the young revolutionaries of Trotsky's generation. The greatest suffering was separation from family and friends. As for the constant police supervision, that too was bearable. The Siberian camps were not yet labour colonies. Books and newspapers were circulated and detainees were able to carry out a certain amount of political work. Even the dread of isolation was evaded: Trotsky and Alexandra married. Soon they had two daughters, Nina and Zina, and moved from the small former mining village of Ust-Kut to Nizhnie-Ilinsk, a much grander metropolis commanding its own doctor. Later they moved to the large town of Verkholensk in north-eastern Siberia.

In Siberia Trotsky began to write on literary matters for the socialist press. His style was genial and humane and he took great delight in reviewing French, Italian and German novels under the pen name 'Antid-Otto' (from the Italian for 'antidote'). For the *Eastern Review* he wrote about the Siberian peasantry and the condition of women. His literary essays discussed the works of the German philosopher Friedrich Nietzsche (1844–1900) and the German author Gerhart Hauptmann (1862–1946), the French novelists Émile Zola (1840–1902) and Guy de Maupassant (1850–93), the Norwegian playwright Henrik Ibsen (1828–1906), the Italian novelist Gabriele D'Annunzio (1863–1938), the English art critic John Ruskin (1819–1900) and from Russia the novelist Nikolai Vasilievich Gogol (1809–52), the philosopher Alexander Ivanovich Herzen (1812–70), the literary critic Vissarion Grigorevich Belinsky (1811–48), the poet Alexander Dobrolyubov (b. 1876), the author Gleb Ivanovich Uspensky (1843–1902), the novelist Maxim Gorky (1868–1936) and many others. At its height, Trotsky's journalism was bringing in the welcome sum of 60 rou-

Born in Constantinople of Jewish middle-class parents, Julius Martov (1873-1923) began his revolutionary activity in St Petersburg, where he founded the Jewish Bund and worked with Lenin and Plekhanov on the *Iskra* newspaper. Martov was close to Trotsky, but turned down the younger man's repeated calls for an anti-war bloc. He opposed the First World War, but stopped short of Lenin's demands for a civil war. These arguments for unity were repeated in the aftermath of the 1917 Revolution. Trotsky expected Martov to join an all-socialist ministry, but Martov refused, protesting against the toppling of Kerensky's Provisional Government. He left Russia for the last time in 1921 and died in exile in Germany.

bles a month. The authorities responded by banning his articles.

Trotsky was a voracious reader. He devoured novels and books on science, politics and even religion. It was in exile that he began to read Darwin and he would later take a close interest in the Austrian psychoanalyst Sigmund Freud (1856–1939). He learned the names of the great European agitators, journalists and politicians and for the first time he read Karl Marx's *Capital*, brushing the cockroaches off the pages as he went.

He also took part in discussion groups, where news reached him that a Russian Social Democratic and Labour Party (RSDLP) had just had its first congress in Minsk in 1898. Written by the future renegade Peter Struve, the party's manifesto began: 'The farther we go to the East of Europe, the more cowardly and dishonest, in a political sense, do we find the bourgeoisie; and the greater, correspondingly, becomes the political and cultural task confronting the proletariat.'[23] Yet despite these proud words, the congress was only a partial success. The delegates were all arrested and the idea of a single Marxist party that would enjoy the support of local groups all over Russia remained little more than a dream.

In Siberia Trotsky received copies of *Iskra* ('*The Spark*'), a radical Marxist magazine being edited from London. Its leading contributors included the great names of Plekhanov's circle: the old man himself, Paul Axelrod and Vera Zasulich, as well as two unfamiliar signatures, Vladimir Lenin and Julius Martov. Lenin had joined the ranks of the Russian Marxists in 1893 and argued in his early articles and books that Russia was already exhibiting signs of capitalism. He also believed there was no possibility of reconstructing society as some sort of enormous peasant commune of the sort proposed by the agrarian populists. Lenin regarded himself as an orthodox Marxist in the style of Plekhanov or his German counterpart Karl Kautsky.

Karl Kautsky (1854–1938) was regarded as the leading interpreter of Marx's legacy. He earned this reputation by publishing summaries of Marx's economic thought. Kautsky then solidified his situation by writing polemics against the 'revisionist' right wing of German socialism. He rejected the First World War, but did not risk damaging party unity by making his opposition public, at least not until the war was under way. He was one of the most public opponents of the Russian Revolution, drawing the wrath of Lenin and Trotsky, who had previously regarded him highly.

Julius Martov was slightly younger than his close friend Lenin. In October 1895 he formed the Struggle for the Emancipation of the Working Classes, better known as the Jewish Bund. Forced to leave Russia, Martov joined several other exiles on the editorial board of *Iskra*. Plekhanov was initially suspicious of Martov (as he was of the younger generation in general), but the old man was eventually won round. Martov's genius lay in the breadth of his reading and in his extraordinary cultural knowledge. He was not in any sense charismatic, however, and had to be coaxed out of his shell. A thin, bearded figure with a weak voice, he often seemed exhausted on the platform and would lose himself in details. It was only in the cut-and-thrust of polemical debate that he shone. While much of Lenin's journalism was restricted to the most immediate practical questions facing workers, Martov, like Trotsky, had a literary style that was more acceptable to a refined, intellectual audience.

In exile Trotsky acquired a copy of Lenin's famous pamphlet *What Is to Be Done?* (1902). Many years later this text would be presented as the great manifesto of 'Leninism' and the clearest expression of his revolutionary ideas. For the Revolution to progress, Lenin argued, the socialist party had to recruit revolutionary activists, workers who could see as clearly as anyone else the economic struggle, but were prepared to use it to raise bigger political questions. Revolutionaries should be 'tribunes of the people', capable of converting other workers to socialism. In fact, much of what Lenin said was unexceptional, but it served to explain to new members of the party the structures that Russian socialists had already been using for a decade or more.

However, there were passages in *What Is to Be Done?* that proved controversial in later years. If the Tsarist police state was ever going to be defeated, Lenin argued, its adversaries had to stay focused and organized. They had to operate as a single, centralized bloc. 'I assert: (1) that no revolutionary movement can endure without a stable organization of leaders maintaining continuity; (2) that the broader the popular mass drawn spontaneously into the struggle, which forms the basis of the movement, and participates in it, the more urgent the need for such an organization and the more solid this organization must be (for it is much easier for all sorts of demagogues to side-track the more backward sections of the masses); (3) that such an organization must consist chiefly of people professionally engaged in revolutionary activity.'[24]

At times Lenin seems to be saying that the party is divided between workers and intellectuals. The workers alone cannot grasp the full range of socialist ideas, so they need the intellectuals to instruct them. But surely this argument carries the germs of a new kind of class snobbery? In his defence, Lenin points out that Tsarism is a total system of state repression and it will not be defeated without a strong, centralized fighting organization. He meant nothing grander than that.[25] Such debates as these did not yet concern Trotsky,[26] although he was aware that a new generation was emerging to take control of the socialist movement.

For all the comparative 'freedom' dissidents enjoyed in Siberia, their lives were carefully monitored and Trotsky had had enough. He escaped in some style, hiding under bales of straw in a peasant's wagon as it trundled out of Verkholensk. He then travelled in disguise to Irkutsk in eastern Siberia and from there to Samara on the Volga River. His passport was so badly forged that he had to fill in his own details, at which point he adopted his

In *What Is to Be Done?* Lenin rejected the idea that all that was needed was for workers to oppose their bosses. Why join a revolutionary socialist party rather than a trade union? His answer was that the trade union movement stopped short of revolution. He also argued that serious revolutionary politics requires discipline and organization. The party needed an elected leadership and a newspaper. Between congresses, its ranks should agree to work under the direction of their leaders. Much later, Lenin's pamphlet would be interpreted as a recipe for dictatorship, but in 1902 it was seen as making the case for an organized socialist revolution.

famous pseudonym 'Trotsky' for the first time (he borrowed it from one of his Odessa jailors). While taking care to dodge train guards and police spies, 'Leon Trotsky' whiled away the long journey reading Homer in Russian translation.

In Samara he joined *Iskra*'s organization, writing under the pseudonym 'Pero' ('The Pen'). He then travelled eastwards on a speaking tour of the Ukraine, visiting Kharkov, Poltava and Kiev until he reached the Russian border. Trotsky was conducted across the frontier by a young Narodnik student who accused him of betraying the principles of the populist movement. 'Did you know that the last issue of *Iskra* featured a shameful polemic against terrorism?' he asked. He even threatened not to help Trotsky, but relented in the end.[27]

Sadly, Trotsky's heroic escape meant permanent separation from Alexandra and his daughters, who were still in Verkholensk. *For several days after I had escaped*, he wrote, *she concealed my absence from the police. From abroad I could hardly keep up a correspondence with her. Then she was exiled for a second time; after this we met only occasionally. Life separated us, but nothing could destroy our friendship and our intellectual kinship.*[28]

One of Trotsky's biographers, Isaac Deutscher, imagines this parting through Alexandra's eyes: 'Alexandra had no doubt that her husband was destined for greatness and that at 23 it was time for him to do something for immortality. She urged him to try to escape from Siberia and in doing so she shouldered the burden of a heavy sacrifice. She had just given birth to their second daughter and was now undertaking to struggle for her own and her children's lives, unaided, with no certainty of a reunion. In her own conviction she was, as a wife and as a revolutionary, merely doing her duty; and she took her duty for granted without the slightest suggestion of melodrama.'[29]

Safely in Europe, Trotsky introduced himself to the leading figures of the Socialist International, including Victor Adler (1852–1918), one of the leaders of Austrian socialism. Arriving in London in October 1902, Trotsky made straight for Lenin's home. It was almost dawn when he knocked on the door, but the author of *What Is to Be Done?* was delighted to meet this energetic 23 year old who told him all about the terrible conditions faced by revolutionaries in Russia. 'The Pen has arrived!' he announced to his wife, Nadezhda, who was also called upon to pay Trotsky's cab fare.

Soon afterwards Lenin took his new friend to see the sights of London. *He showed me Westminster – the exterior – and other remarkable buildings. I do not remember literally his expressions, but the meaning was such: 'Here is* their *famous Westminster.' This word designated not the English, but the enemy. This accent was clearly underlined, deeply organic and found expression through the pitch of the voice. This was always the one that Lenin chose when he spoke about cultural wealth, new conquests, the British Museum, the rich information of* The Times, *or many years after, of German artillery, of French aviation: 'They know, they have, they make, they obtain – but what enemies!' The imperceptible shade of the exploiting class seemed to cover in his eyes all culture. This shadow, he saw unceasingly and as clear as daylight.*[30]

Lenin's wife Nadezhda Krupskaya (1869–1939) trained as a teacher giving evening classes to workers. She followed Lenin into exile and served the revolutionary government as the Commissar for Adult Education. After Lenin's death she tried and failed to secure the publication of his Testament, which criticized Stalin.

Trotsky's dramatic escape from Siberia opened up new possibilities. He was young and talented and his elder comrades made good use of his skills. He was quickly introduced to the leading circles of the exiled socialist press and Lenin encouraged him to help edit *Iskra,* although others, notably Plekhanov, remained wary and aloof: why was Lenin spending so much time with this young Trotsky? Martov, too, was just as friendly as Lenin and Trotsky admired them both.

Through his journalism Trotsky soon acquired a formidable reputation and was invited to speak in France, Switzerland and Belgium. Various clandestine groups in Russia also demanded that he return and help them overthrow Nicholas II, but Lenin campaigned to keep his young comrade by his side. Uncertain about his future, Trotsky made his way to Paris to address several groups of Russian exiles and to listen to the French socialist Jean Jaurès (1859–1914). *For the first time, I came face to face with real art,* he recalled later, having visited the Louvre and attended the Opéra.[31] In Paris he also fell in love again. Natalia Sedova was a good match and they eventually married, staying together for the rest of Trotsky's life and having two sons, Sergei and Sedov.

The second Congress of the Russian Social Democratic and Labour Party (RSDLP) was held in London in 1903. It was a disaster from the start when the Jewish Bund walked out, but some-

Trotsky's second wife Natalia Sedova (1882–1962) worked with her husband and Lenin on the newspaper *Iskra*. Their two sons were killed in the 1930s during Stalin's purges of the opposition. Throughout the 1920s and 1930s Natalia wrote for such publications as Trotsky's *Bulletin*. In 1951 she broke with the surviving members of the Fourth International, citing the Trotskyists' failure to criticize Russian imperialism in Eastern Europe and the lack of democracy within the International.

thing crucial also happened. The RSDLP split into two factions: the Bolsheviks (meaning the 'majority') and the Mensheviks (the 'minority'). There would be no reconciliation for many years to come. At the head of the Bolsheviks was Lenin. Leading the Mensheviks was Martov, with whom Trotsky initially sided.

Two major issues split the RSDLP. The first was the nature of party organization. At the London congress Lenin had argued that membership of the party should be restricted to those who worked under the direction of its leading organization (this quickly became known as 'democratic centralism'). Naturally the Party would take decisions in as democratic a manner as possible, but once a decision had been made all comrades would be expected to implement it, even if they had previously been opposed. This conception of inner-party democracy angered the Mensheviks, including Trotsky, who thought the source of this dispute was in fact Lenin's pamphlet *What Is to Be Done?*

In Trotsky's view, Lenin's position would lead to a situation in which the leading figures of the party could dominate its members. Where had the idea that the workers could learn from the intellectuals come from? Surely Marx had learned from workers' uprisings such as the Paris Commune? Lenin was being elitist. What would happen if a Leninist party came to power? How could it spread democracy when it was so blatantly undemocratic? In a 1904 article, Trotsky warned that Lenin's 'democratic centralism' would lead to a situation of terror in which *the organiza-*

tion of the Party substitutes itself for the Party as a whole; then the Central Committee substitutes itself for the organization; and finally 'the dictator' substitutes himself for the Central Committee.[33] This is, in fact, exactly what happened; but in the 1920s Trotsky's critics used these prescient remarks against him, claiming he was a Menshevik after all.

The second issue that drove a wedge between the Bolsheviks and the Mensheviks was not immediately obvious, but it became clearer over time. Martov's democratic formulations were supported not just by fiery revolutionaries like Trotsky, but by moderates in the party. Gradually, Menshevism drifted away from revolutionary idealism to a more modest and pragmatic reformism. When this became apparent, several Mensheviks left to join Lenin and the Bolsheviks; others tried to mediate between the two factions. Lenin's allies argued that the Mensheviks were 'opportunists' and that their commitment to revolution was limited.

Trotsky came to much the same opinion. He tried to break with Martov in 1904, but rather than admit their differences the Mensheviks refused to publish his letters. Nevertheless, long after he had split from the Mensheviks, Trotsky always portrayed himself as a 'conciliator' between the two sides. He knew that these factions made little sense to anyone outside the party and he always maintained that a united party with diverse tendencies would be far more successful than a scattering of splinter groups. He also understood the emotional appeal of a truly united social-

The revolutionary Paris Commune in 1871 seized Paris after the French defeat in the Franco-Prussian War (1870–1). Marx supported the Communards, though doubted they would survive. This was an important influence on Lenin, who wrote that 'the Commune was lost because it compromised and reconciled'. For every day of the Russian Revolution that lasted longer than the Commune, Lenin declared 'Commune plus one', or 'Commune plus two . . .' and at his death his body was wrapped in a Communard flag. [32]

Rosa Luxemburg and Karl Liebknecht in Leipzig 1909

Revisionism. Since the re-foundation of the Socialist International in 1889, the largest bloc of opinion in socialist Europe had remained loyally Marxist. The largest left-wing party was the German Social Democratic Party (SPD), whose leadership included men such as Engels, Kautsky and Eduard Bernstein (1850–1932). Following Engels's death in 1895,

three blocs of opinion formed. On the right, Bernstein maintained that Marx had been wrong to predict the demise of capitalism. He supported the demands of moderate trade unionists and argued that Germany should keep her colonies. Bernstein elaborated a programme for parliamentary socialism that was followed for the next 100 years.

ist front. For all these reasons, he wanted the Bolsheviks and the Mensheviks to make peace.

The conflicts within Russian Marxism were not exclusive to Russia. They reflected disputes within the international workers' movement, which was rapidly splitting into three camps: the 'revisionist' right; the 'centre'; and the revolutionary 'left'. Lenin's allies associated the Mensheviks with the Right, claiming they were minorities in Europe and Russia. Meanwhile, Martov and his allies accused the Bolsheviks of combining near-anarchist ideas about the possibility of revolution with authoritarian solutions to the problems of party democracy. They quoted Plekhanov's jibe against Lenin during the 1903 Congress: 'Robespierres are made of this!'[34] The reference was not to the revolutionary Robespierre of 1792, but to the dictator of 1793 and the man blamed for the French Terror. Who in their right mind would fight the Tsar only to create another dictator?

The Centre. In the centre of European socialism, Karl Kautsky defended the original arguments of Marx. Capital was becoming better organized, as was its antagonist, the proletariat. To such people as the young Russian Marxists Lenin, Martov and Trotsky, Kautsky was an impressive figure, holding out for Marxist orthodoxy and refuting the challenge of the right. But the facts worked in Bernstein's favour, not Kautsky's: the formation of mass unions with conservative leaderships, the growth of bureaucratic parties with much to lose, the adaptation of socialist deputies to nationalism. Even Kautsky postponed the revolution to some indefinite date in the future.

It is often said that Trotsky became a Menshevik in 1903 and remained one all of his life – an argument used against him in the dark months following Lenin's death, when the whole party seemed to turn against the 'newcomer'. In his memoirs, Trotsky dodged the charge, insisting that he had broken from Martov within a year of the schism in the party. *Of the* Iskra *editors,* he wrote, *my closest connections were with Martov, Zasulich and Axelrod.*

The Left. Rosa Luxemburg (1870–1919) attacked Bernstein's claim that capitalism could be reformed and accused Kautsky of dodging the question of whether socialists should pursue reform or revolution. In the run-up to 1914, small groups of socialists impatient for change began to identify with revolutionaries like Luxemburg rather than ambiguous figures like Kautsky. This revolutionary left would later form the backbone of the *Zimmerwald* peace movement and of the Communist International from 1919.

Their influence over me was unquestionable. Before the congress there were various shades of opinion on the editorial board, but no sharp differences. I stood farthest from Plekhanov, who, after the first really trivial encounters, had taken an intense dislike to me. Lenin's attitude towards me was unexceptionally kind. But now it was he who, in my eyes, was attacking the editorial board, a body which was, in my opinion, a single unit and which bore the exciting name of Iskra. *The idea of a split within the board seemed nothing short of sacrilegious to me.*[35]

That is Trotsky's version, but the truth is more complex. The Mensheviks and the Bolsheviks were not clearly distinguished. Plekhanov, later a figure on the socialist right, supported Lenin against Martov in 1903. Meanwhile, others who are usually associated with the Bolshevik left voted at first with the Menshevik right. Trotsky was not alone in misunderstanding the dispute. It would be too easy, however, to pretend – as Trotsky sometimes did – that his identification with Martov was short-lived. In his last years, Trotsky often wondered why it was that Martov had not lived up to the revolutionary ferments of 1905 and 1917. What was the source of Lenin's genius? How had he been able to grasp the possibilities of the situation? The answer, he realized, was Lenin's use of Marxist dialectic.

Martov sometimes very intelligently analysed regroupings in the sphere of parliamentary politics, changes in the tendencies of the Press, the manoeuvres of ruling circles – insofar as all this was limited to ongoing politics, the preparatory stage for distant events or the peaceful conditions when only the leaders, deputies, journalists and ministers of pre-war Europe acted in the political arena, when the basic antagonists remained virtually unchanging. Within these boundaries Martov swam about like a fish in water. His dialectic was a dialectic of derivative processes and limited scale, episodic changes. Beyond these boundaries he did not venture.

On the contrary, Lenin's dialectic had a massive character. His thought – his opponents often accused him of this 'simplified' reality, indeed swept aside the secondary and episodic in

The doctrine of dialectical materialism was first associated with the German philosopher G W F Hegel (1770–1831), but was later developed by Engels to become part of the wider notion of historical materialism. The notion of dialectic expresses the view that development depends on the clash of contradictions and the creation of a new, more advanced synthesis. The dialectical process involves the three moments: thesis, antithesis and synthesis. Marx used the notion to account for social and historical events.

order to deal with the basic. Thus, Engels 'simplified' reality when he defined the State as armed detachments of people with material appendages in the form of jails. But this was a saving simplification: *true, insufficient in itself for an evaluation of the conjunctures of the day, it was decisive in the last historical analysis. Lenin's thought operated with living classes as the basic factors of society and thus revealed* all *its power in those periods when the great masses entered the scene, that is, in periods of profound upheavals, wars and revolutions. The Leninist dialectic was a dialectic for the grand scale.*[36]

Trotsky's argument united each man's psychology with observable fact. His explanation of the different roles played by Lenin and Martov was not founded simply in the character of either man, but in the situation around them. The point to notice, however, is not so much Trotsky's 'answer' as his question. Why was Trotsky so concerned to explain the collapse of Martov's revolutionary views? One reason was Trotsky's sense that he had backed the wrong man in 1903. Only later would he have a chance to choose again.

In the meantime, however, it was not obvious that the 1903 schism would last. The hold of Tsarism was weakening and socialists enjoyed unprecedented influence. Within two years of the London Congress, events had pushed the Bolsheviks and Mensheviks back together and old divisions were forgotten as Russia entered a new period of revolt.

The Dress Rehearsal (1904–1916)

The background to the troubles lay in Russia's war against Japan, which began in February 1904. Nicholas II's forces were tied up in Manchuria, thousands of miles from central Russia and hindered by the fact that the Trans-Siberian Railway was still incomplete. In July the unpopular and reactionary Minister of the Interior, Viacheslav Plehve, was assassinated. From exile, Trotsky wrote: *Our ships are slow. Our guns do not fire far enough. Our soldiers are illiterate. Our NCOs have neither map nor compass. Our soldiers go barefoot, naked and hungry. Our Red Cross steals. Our supply services steal . . . Years of peaceful propaganda could not achieve what one day of war does.*[37]

In autumn 1904 Trotsky and Natalia stayed in Munich with Alexander Helphand, another *Iskra* journalist who went by the nickname 'Parvus'. Parvus was a complex figure. He had a face like a bulldog and was an advocate of the most militant tactics. Yet Parvus was also a chancer. He told Trotsky he wanted money to fund a newspaper that could carry the revolutionary message in three languages, but later he dropped out of radical politics. In 1904–5, however, Parvus had experience on his side and his prediction of an imminent revolt in Russia convinced the young Trotsky.

Soon after the Russo-Japanese war began, Parvus published a series of articles in which he predicted that the long period of European tranquillity, which had lasted since the Franco-German peace of 1871, was now coming

An intermediary between the German and Russian socialists, Alexander Helphand or 'Parvus' (1868–1924) took part in the 1905 Soviet or workers' council. His arguments helped Trotsky to clarify his own ideas. Parvus later became an arms dealer and a supporter of the German war. Lenin refused him entry to Russia after the Revolution.

In 1891 work began on a railway across Siberia, linking Russia with the Pacific Ocean and China. The Russians obtained Beijing's permission to run a segment of the Trans-Siberian Railway across Chinese Manchuria, but in 1903 Nicholas II decided to annex Manchuria. The Japanese, who had designs on the area, conceded Manchuria to Russia in return for Russia's recognition of their claim to Korea. The Russians rejected this and in February 1904 Japan attacked the naval base of Port Arthur (now Lüda), which Russia had leased from China. The Japanese quickly neutralized Russia's Pacific Fleet and secured mastery of the China Sea. In January 1905 Port Arthur fell and in May the Japanese sank the Baltic and Black Sea fleets, forcing Russia's surrender. With US President Theodore Roosevelt (1858–1919) as intermediary, Russia negotiated a peace treaty.

to an end. Competition for raw materials and colonies was driving the world towards war, he said, but the workers of Europe would inevitably choose peace over war. 'The worldwide process of capitalist development leads to a political upheaval in Russia. This in turn must have its impact on the political development of all capitalist countries. The Russian Revolution will shake the bourgeois world. And the Russian proletariat may well play the role of the vanguard of the socialist revolution.' [38] Such arguments as these helped Trotsky to develop his journalism into formed theses.

The 1905 Revolution began properly on 9 January when the Tsar's troops opened fire on a loyal demonstration of St Petersburg workers, killing hundreds. 'Bloody Sunday', as it became known, drove Russia's workers to protest as never before. The number of strikes in January and February of that year was higher than in all the previous ten years combined. In the months that followed, the cities were convulsed as millions of workers went on strike for the democratization of the regime, while in the countryside the peasants sacked the estates of the landlords. Trotsky was one of the first exiles to return to Russia. He spoke from public plat-

'Bloody Sunday' Soldiers fire on fleeing protestors in the Winter Palace Square January 1905

In January 1905 some 120,000 workers went on strike in protest at the dismissal of several workers from the largest industrial plant in St Petersburg. Permission was granted for a procession to present the Tsar with a petition of grievances, provided they did not come near the Winter Palace. On Sunday 9 January a peaceful demonstration moved through the city, but ran into armed troops barring the way to the Palace. They opened fire, killing 200 and wounding 800.

forms and defied the threat of arrest. One of his closest allies at this time was Leonid Krasin (1870–1926), a member of the Bolshevik Central Committee and a supporter of 'conciliation' between Bolsheviks and Mensheviks.

Krasin published Trotsky's letters and pamphlets on a secret printing press in the Caucasus and they were widely circulated by underground organizations. As a result Trotsky's star rose. The future Bolshevik Commissar for Culture, Anatoly Lunacharsky (1875–1933), describes Trotsky's success at this time. 'I must say that of all the social-democratic leaders of 1905–6 Trotsky undoubtedly showed himself, despite his youth, to be the best prepared. Less than any of them did he bear the stamp of a certain kind of émigré narrowness of outlook, which . . . even affected Lenin at that time. Trotsky . . . emerged from the Revolution having acquired an enormous degree of popularity, whereas neither Lenin nor Martov had effectively gained at all. Plekhanov had lost a great deal, thanks to his display of quasi-Kadet tendencies. Trotsky stood then in the very front rank.'[39]

Russia's Marxist factions responded to the 1905 Revolution in different ways. In *Iskra*, for instance, Martov called on Russian businesses to embrace democracy in emulation of their Western counterparts. The Mensheviks supported the mass revolution, but their strategy was to hold back protests – the workers could be satisfied once democracy had been achieved. In contrast, the Bolsheviks were unwilling to work with other groups, which proved limiting as the workers began to organize for themselves. Only in the autumn of 1905 did this change, as Lenin urged his comrades to break down the suffocating hold of the older comrades and open up the party to the energy of new members.

Meanwhile the workers' uprising continued to grow. On 10 October a rail strike spread throughout the country. On 13 October a workers' council or 'soviet' was established for the first time in St Petersburg. It became an alternative assembly of trade

In October 1905 a number of strikers and their supporters agreed to meet regularly. The St Petersburg Soviet was a working-class institution that gained great popular legitimacy during the strikes. The Soviet organized street patrols to prevent looting and a press to report on the strike. It even took over the running of the postal service and railways. In 1917 this model was adopted all over Russia. In every city revolutionary councils were established on a delegate basis, with elections held in large workplaces and the nominees subject to recall at any moment. These soviets debated all the immediate, practical questions that mattered to people in that area, such as food distribution and basic services, and the Bolsheviks saw them as the potential basis for a new workers' state.

The October Revolution. Protestors march on the Nevsky Prospect St Petersburg 1905

unions, workers' parties and other representatives. Trotsky was soon elected to the presidency and the movement prepared for revolution. But even as the rail strike began, the Tsar was already looking for means to re-establish his authority. On 17 October he published a manifesto establishing a limited parliament or Duma. It was to be advisory in character and elected on an indirect representative basis, weighting the votes heavily in favour of the privileged few. Liberals like Peter Struve claimed that Russia's freedom had arrived. The Mensheviks argued that workers' parties should stand for election. The Bolsheviks and Trotsky called for a boycott.

Nicholas II's manifesto also included a limited amnesty for political exiles and many socialists returned to Russia. Those such as Lenin or Martov who hoped to claim leadership found Trotsky had got there before them. In fact, Martov complained throughout the 1905 Revolution of an inability to think clearly or to impose himself on events. Perhaps it was neurasthenia or mental fatigue, although Trotsky was more scathing. *Martov did not know what to call his illness*, he wrote, *but it has a definite name:* Menshevism. *In an epoch of revolution, opportunism means, first of all, vacillation.*[40]

The St Petersburg Soviet existed for 50 days. It was strong enough to frighten the regime, but too weak to overthrow it. In December 1905 the Tsar's troops invaded the Soviet, although Trotsky, who was chairing a meeting, made them wait until a final resolution had been passed.

The leaders of the Soviet went on trial, accused of stockpiling arms and preparing an insurrection. The case generated wide publicity and Trotsky was even photographed in his cell. He gave his final speech to the court secure in the knowledge that he would be regarded throughout Europe as one of the greatest rebels of the age. He also ridiculed the idea that a handful of leaders were responsible for the mass protest that Russia had just witnessed. *A rising of the masses is not made*, he told the judges. *It makes itself of its own accord. It is the result of social relations and not of a scheme drawn up on paper. A popular insurrection cannot be staged. It can only be foreseen. For reasons that were as little dependent on us as on Tsarism, an open conflict has become inevitable . . . no matter how important the weapons may be, it is not to them, gentlemen the judges, that great power resides. No! Not the ability of the masses to kill others, but their great readiness themselves to die, this secures in the last instance the victory of the popular uprising.*[41]

Trotsky's speech was generally well received. *My mother was sure that I would not only be acquitted, but even given some mark of distinction*, he observed later. *I tried to prepare her for a sentence to hard labour.*[42] Trotsky was right. He was sentenced to lifelong exile in Siberia, a tougher sentence than the last. He would be taken to the deserted reaches of the empire and kept under close supervision until the day he died.

As before, however, exile at least provided Trotsky with an opportunity to write. In *1905* (1907) he described the Tsarist

Trotsky's theory of permanent revolution was a response to the contradictions faced by Russian Marxists. Russia had one of the most vibrant protest movements in Europe, but the left-wing nature of its socialism was not the product of social development. The majority of people lived on the land, while the Tsar ruled as a dictator. Russian Marxism traditionally argued that any state could not leap straight from feudalism to socialism or Communism. The progress from one form of society to another depended on the level of production and the general development of the economy and society. The most socialists could expect from any radical advance would be the creation of a bourgeoisie that might evolve towards socialism over many years. Trotsky rejected this argument in 1905 because it assumed that any revolution would have to be limited. What would happen, though, if the revolution spread across national borders? He argued that one way to create socialism in Russia would be if whole parts of Europe turned to revolution. The wealth and development of the West would then be allied to the political radicalism of the East and the shift to socialism could happen.

state as being on the verge of collapse. In his analysis, absolutism depended on the exhaustion of the rising capitalist class as it challenged a decaying feudalism. This equilibrium could not last, he predicted, and further revolts would come.

As an appendix to *1905*, he wrote a series of theses – 'Results and Prospects' – elaborating on his ideas. One of them contained the first statement of the theory of permanent revolution, Trotsky's most important contribution to socialist thought. To understand the originality of his argument we need to place his ideas in context. We have already seen that the oldest Russian revolutionary tradition was Narodism. The populists maintained that the conditions already existed in Russia for a different society based on the existing collective structures in the countryside.

Russian Marxists were critical of this view. Marx himself had argued that men and women did not make history just as they pleased, but in conditions inherited from the past and therefore limited by history. Socialism was supposed to create a society of plenty. How could it be achieved in a backward country without sufficient material resources? This had been the argument between Trotsky and Alexandra Sokolovskaya in the 1890s. The early Russian Marxists had concluded that Russia must live through a capitalist stage before moving on to socialism. (Even after 1905, the Mensheviks continued to argue this position.) If another revolution broke out, they said, its leaders should counsel the workers to wait. Russia was still a feudal society and the task of the revolution could only be to speed up the development of capitalism. Democracy could be achieved, but not socialism. After the Tsar, it would be the liberals' turn to rule.

For many socialists this position was untenable. Had the revolution not shown that millions of workers were unwilling to wait? Surely the radicalization of the masses was an objective historical factor? Lenin and the Bolsheviks tried to give a sense of purpose to the left by arguing that the workers did not need to wait for an entire historical epoch to pass before demanding socialism. Russia was underdeveloped economically and the Mensheviks were right to argue that a quick transition to socialism was impossible. But should the workers and peasants rise up again, they would create some sort of alternative, temporary society.

The Bolsheviks had in mind something like the Jacobin Republic of 1793–4. It would enjoy the support of the majority and, although it would not be a socialist regime, within the limits of capitalism it could pass profound, democratic reforms: universal suffrage, the breaking-up of the landlords' estates, the eight-hour day. This goal they termed 'the democratic dictatorship of the proletariat and the peasantry'.

As President of the St Petersburg Soviet, Trotsky had worked far more closely with the Bolsheviks than with his former allies the Mensheviks. But he could not accept their strategy. Instead, he argued for the spreading of the revolution beyond the borders of the existing imperial state. Like the Mensheviks and the Bolsheviks, he accepted that the Russian working class was a minority and that the workers could not rule alone if democracy was to prevail. So with whom should Russia's workers unite? The Mensheviks had identified the Russian capitalists as potential allies and the Bolsheviks had suggested the peasantry, but Trotsky preferred to emphasize the potential role of workers in Western Europe. No capitalist would support socialism, he argued, and no peasant would progress beyond the goal of land redistribution.

In September 1791 King Louis XVI of France accepted a new constitution. However, his lack of co-operation led to the proclamation of a republic and he was executed in 1793. The moderate republican Girondins were ousted by the extremist Jacobins and the power passed to the Committee of Public Safety. Under the revolutionary Maximilien Robespierre (1758–94) the Committee conducted a Reign of Terror in which thousands were executed, including Robespierre.

Only the industrial workforce outside Russia could continue the fight for socialism.

Trotsky borrowed the phrase 'permanent revolution' from an address written by Marx and Engels in 1850: 'It is our interest and our task to make the Revolution permanent, until all more or less possessing classes have been forced out of their position of dominance . . . and the association of proletarians, not only in one country but in all the dominant countries of the world, has advanced so far that . . . the decisive productive forces are concentrated in the hands of the proletariat.'[43]

Here Marx and Engels are concerned with the tasks facing revolutionaries after 1848, when most European countries were still looking to complete their own bourgeois revolution. Fifty years later, Russia was still at the same stage. As ever, the task was to find a means to advance from a bourgeois to a socialist revolution. Trotsky was convinced that any successful Russian revolution would need to spread to the West if it was to survive. Then, as the revolution became permanent in a historic sense it could progress from a bourgeois to a socialist phase. In a united socialist Europe many things might be achieved that would not be possible in an isolated Russian state.[44]

This is how Trotsky later summarized his theory: *The complete victory of the democratic revolution in Russia is conceivable only in the form of the dictatorship of the proletariat, which would inevitably place on the order of the day not only democratic but socialistic tasks as well and would at the same time give a powerful impetus to the international socialist revolution. Only the victory of the proletariat in Russia from bourgeois restoration can assure it the possibility of founding the establishment of socialism.*[45]

In 'Results and Prospects' Trotsky had dealt with the international tasks facing the revolution. They were not discussed abstractly, but were predicted according to the movements he could see around him. First, a second Russian revolution would have an extraordinary impact on neighbouring countries. The Hohenzollern Empire of Germany and the Habsburg Empire of Austria-Hungary would inevitably be dragged in. *The triumph of the Revolution in Russia will mean the inevitable victory of the Revolution in Poland. It is not difficult to imagine that the existence of a revolutionary regime in the ten provinces of Russian Poland must lead to the revolt of Galicia and Poznan. The Hohenzollern and Hapsburg Governments will reply to this by sending military forces to the Polish frontier in order then to cross it for the purpose of crushing their enemy at his very centre – Warsaw . . . What attitude would the Austrian and German proletariat take up then? It is evident that they could not remain calm while the armies of their country were conducting a counterrevolutionary crusade.*[46]

In Trotsky's view, the impact of any successful revolution would be felt far beyond the borders of the European East and would test the limits of parliamentary socialism. *The European Socialist Parties, particularly the largest of them, the German Social Democratic Party, have developed their conservatism in proportion as the great masses have embraced socialism and the more these masses have become organized and disciplined . . . The tremendous influence of the Russian Revolution indicates that it will destroy party routinism and conservatism and place the question of an open trial of strength between the proletariat and capitalist reaction on the order of the day. Should the Russian proletariat find itself in power, if only as the result of a temporary conjuncture of circumstances in our bourgeois revolution, it will encounter the organized hostility of the world reaction and on the other hand will find a readiness on the part of the world proletariat to give organized support.*[47]

These passages are of considerable importance, for after 1917 Trotsky's predictions would be tested by history. Indeed, if politics is only 'concentrated prediction', then this was politics of the highest quality. In all essentials Trotsky read the diplomatic situation right. War was indeed coming and, as he argued, a new Russian revolution would begin and then spread. The only question was: how far?

In later years Trotsky's originality would be used against him. The fact that he (rather than Lenin) had formulated the theory of permanent revolution suggested to many that it was not a truly Bolshevik idea. Some historians have even questioned Trotsky's Marxist pedigree. Surely Marx would never have followed Trotsky in arguing that a world revolution might begin in impoverished Russia? The point of Marx's theory was that socialism should begin in Germany or any of the leading European states.

Yet Marx's attitude towards a possible Russian revolution was far from certain. Several groups of Russian socialists and populists wrote to him in 1877 and 1881 asking for advice. The most famous letter Marx wrote in reply was addressed to Vera Zasulich in 1881 and it has rarely been quoted. He began it three times and each draft has a different emphasis, so that the final tone of Marx's answer amounts to little more than the implied statement 'You decide'. Marx had no notion of how much socialist potential there was in the Russian collective village system; nor was he at that time convinced that capitalism was a necessary stage on the road to revolution. Much to the disappointment of his Russian admirers, Marx was unwilling to draw up a blueprint for their country's future.

Another question he avoided in his correspondence was what sort of strategy should be adopted by socialists in the underdeveloped countries, the so-called Third World? Evidently the despotism of these states would result in protests. So was 'socialism' impossible in societies that had not yet matched the economic development of the West? Trotsky's theory of permanent revolution cut through such questions and showed that there was an alternative to waiting for capitalism to come and then pass. It argued for an alliance between the workers in the richest and poorest nations and it took seriously the last line of *The Communist Manifesto*: 'Workers of the world unite.' Trotsky had *completed* Marx's analysis.

Trotsky's theory of permanent revolution was at the heart of his life's work and is generally regarded as his main contribution to 'the actuality of the Revolution'.[48] But Trotsky's theory, like all theories, belongs to a definite moment in history. By 1906

Nikolai Bukharin economist and editor of the party newspaper Pravda he did not survive the last of the purges in 1938

Nikolai Bukharin (1888–1938) joined the Bolsheviks as a student in 1906 and was repeatedly arrested thereafter. He was a member of the party's political bureau and the executive committee of the Communist International. After the Revolution he was associated with the left-wing Bolsheviks, but later allied himself with the right of the Communist Party. He supported Stalin after Lenin's death and formulated the theory of 'socialism in one country'. At the third public show trial, Bukharin defended himself with dignity, gently mocking his prosecutors while pleading guilty to the most extraordinary, implausible and fantastic crimes. He was found guilty by the court and executed.

Rosa Luxemburg (1871–1919) played a leading role in the Polish and German socialist movements. Her pamphlet *Reform or Revolution* (1900) went further than Kautsky in giving the most compelling case against Bernstein's revisionism. *The Mass Strike, the Political Party and the Unions* (1906) used the 1905 revolution to argue for the radicalizing of German socialism. A leading figure in the German anti-war and revolutionary left, she supported Lenin's October Revolution, while criticizing aspects of Bolshevik policy. She helped to found the Spartacus League, which became the German Communist Party. She was arrested and murdered by soldiers after the abortive German Revolution of 1919.

Marxist theory was in a weak condition and the dominant ideas were those of the Second International. In the hands of such writers as Kautsky, Marxism had been purged of its creative energy. The history of the world was said to progress according to inexorable laws that had been well documented. Everything was fixed like clockwork and each nation had to progress steadily through certain established stages. Change was never sudden, but occurred almost mechanically through an incredibly slow process of social and economic evolution.

Trotsky's theory of permanent revolution was the first of a wave of revolutionary insights that challenged and eventually destroyed the Marxism of the Second International. There was Lenin's rediscovery of Hegelian dialectics in 1914 and also Nikolai Bukharin and Rosa Luxemburg's theories of imperialism and the world economy. Common to all these arguments were two insights. First, the capitalist world is a total system that cannot be understood simply by adding up the conditions within existing states. Relations between states and indeed the laws of the system as a whole are equally important. Second, there is no rule saying that capitalism should remain for the indefinite future or even that the capitalism of the future will resemble its present form. Such theories as permanent revolution restore the revolutionary content of Marxism. At a theoretical level, it prepared the ground for the great practical advance of October 1917.

Trotsky was in exile when he put the finishing touches to his theory of permanent revolution. The first eight years of his political activity had been tremendously exciting. Small groups of intellectuals had formulated new ideas that had gone on to capture the hearts and minds of the masses. But these successes had been followed by a harsh reminder of Tsarist rule. Repression had been re-established and racist gangs conducted pogroms against the Jews, who were blamed for the 1905 uprising. One of the worst affected cities was Odessa, where dozens were killed.

Two parliaments were elected in Moscow with a significant populist bloc, the Social Revolutionaries (SRs) standing as Trudoviks or 'Labour'. But Nicholas II's new Minister of the Interior, Pyotr Stolypin (1862–1911), dissolved the parliament and passed new laws reducing popular representation. Opportunities for socialists to stand as candidates were severely reduced.

This was also a bitter time internationally. Wars broke out in Southern Europe and every month brought more news of gathering tensions between the great powers.

Another casualty of this period was any hope of reconciliation between the Bolsheviks and Mensheviks. The split had begun in earnest in the summer of 1903, but the 1905 Revolution had reunited the two factions in a shared desire to push the Revolution to its limits. The next seven years saw more periods of semi-unity (1906–7 and 1910–12) and of inner-party hostility (1908–9). With the mass movement in retreat, a significant number of Mensheviks agued for a strategy of legality. Radicals, they said, should make peace with the more liberal aspects of the Tsar's regime. A Bolshevik minority lurched in the opposite direction towards covert action such as robbing banks and strikes against military and economic targets. The year 1912 saw yet another split between these two sides.[49]

Pyotr Stolypin the Tsar's Minister of the Interior he was assassinated in 1911

Meanwhile Trotsky had once again tired of captivity and decided to escape from Siberia. This time he was being guarded more carefully – even his guards were supervised by yet more guards. The state had chosen to banish him to Berezov, deep in the Siberian wilderness. *For hundreds of miles*, wrote Trotsky, *there are no police and not a single Russian settlement, only occasional Ostyak huts. No sign of a telegraph. There are no horses along the entire route, as the track is exclusively for deer travel. The police could not overtake one, but there was the possibility of getting lost in the wilderness and perishing in the snow.*[50] Nevertheless, he eventually found a sympathetic, if alcoholic, sled driver who was prepared to help him escape. They travelled for seven days, covering 700 kilometres, before arriving at the Ural Mountains. The newspapers were full of Trotsky's exploits, reporting that he was headed for Russia's arctic North. On the contrary, he made for St Petersburg and escaped from there to Finland.[51]

He could no longer live in Russia. Instead he travelled to London, Paris, Vienna and Berlin where he was supported by some of the most prominent names of the European left. He later recalled visiting a Berlin café where he had an opportunity to listen in on a conversation between three socialist MPs: the German Eduard Bernstein, the Austrian Rudolf Hilferding (1877–1941) and Ramsay MacDonald (1866–1937), who would later be the first British Labour prime minister. He listened in silence and found their discussion horribly trite.

On his way through Europe, however, Trotsky was able to meet his family again, albeit briefly. *My father learned to spell out words even when he was quite an old man, in order to be able to read at least the titles of my books. I followed him with excitement in Berlin in 1910, when he perseveringly tried to understand my book on German Social Democracy.*[52]

Short of money, he took paid work as a journalist and was briefly a war correspondent in Yugoslavia for a Kiev newspaper.[53] It seemed the whole of Europe was in danger of following the Slavs towards war. On his journeys Trotsky met members of the Balkan left, who bravely spoke out against nationalism and war. During this period he made one of his most enduring friendships, with Christian Rakovsky (1873–1941), a linguist and doctor who led the Romanian socialist party.

In 1912 Russia was hit by a new wave of strikes in protest against the massacre of gold miners at Lena in Siberia. Suddenly the workers' movement revived and took an upward turn, although two years later, when the First World War broke out, it came to an abrupt halt. The Socialist International had long pledged to meet any outbreak of war with strikes and revolutions, and Russian revolutionaries were convinced the workers' movement would act to prevent a war.

In fact, the International capitulated. After a right-wing gunman assassinated Jean Jaurès, the leader of the French socialist party, French and German deputies voted to support war budgets rather than stand up for their beliefs. In the absence of any alternative from their socialist leaders, large numbers of men volunteered to serve their country in the war. There was a resurgence of nationalism throughout Europe. In 1914 St Petersburg was renamed Petrograd, to sound more Russian (it became Leningrad in 1924), while in London German shops were destroyed by angry mobs.

Trotsky was in Vienna with the Austrian socialist Victor Adler on 2 August 1914 when the news reached him that Germany had declared war on France. *On the way to the prefecture in the motorcar I drew Adler's attention to the fact that in Vienna the war had brought to the surface a sort of festive mood. 'Those who are celebrating are the ones who don't have to go to war,' he answered, 'and their joy seems to be patriotic now. What is more, at present all the unbalanced and all the insane are coming out on the streets: this is their day. But serious people are sitting at home in a state of alarm . . . Jaurès' assassination is just the beginning. War throws open the field to every instinct and every type of lunacy.'*[54]

To Trotsky, these words already seemed inadequate. Should socialists just stay at home, waiting for the horror to blow over? Or should they argue and campaign against the war? But there were other more immediate considerations: *Heyer, the chief of the political police, suggested that an order might be made the following morning for the detention of Russians and Serbs under guard.*[55] Within three hours he had escaped on a train to neutral Switzerland.

Trotsky witnessed the early months of the war from Paris, alongside a circle of left-wing French writers and activists including Alfred Rosmer (1885–1971) and Pierre Monatte (1881–1960). These two socialists were in fact revolutionary syndicalists in favour of transferring the ownership and control of the means of production and distribution to workers' unions. They believed that the trade unions should fight a war against capitalism and that once it had been won the unions could form the basis of a new, equal society. They contributed with Trotsky to a Russian-language publication, *Nashe Slovo,* and later played a leading role in the Red International of Labour Unions – the early 1920s, alliance of Bolshevik trade unionists and revolutionary syndicalists in France, Italy, Spain and elsewhere.

Despite such contacts, Trotsky was astonished and dismayed at the demise of what had been a large and confident anti-war left. *There were elements of opposition scattered about*, he wrote in his autobiography, *but they showed few signs of life.*[56] It was infuriating and not a little depressing for others, too. When Lenin was handed a newspaper stating that the German socialists had voted for war, he insisted it was a forgery. Neither Lenin nor Trotsky had been prepared for such a betrayal.

In heated debates among Russian émigrés, Trotsky continued to work for reconciliation between Martov's Mensheviks and Lenin's Bolsheviks. The Bolshevik playwright and future commissar Lunacharsky describes one such attempt, which took place in Paris in 1915. 'We sincerely wanted to bring about, on a new basis of internationalism, the complete unification of our Party front all the way from Lenin to Martov,' he recalled. 'I spoke up for this course in the most energetic fashion . . . Trotsky fully associated himself with this. It had long been his dream and it seemed to justify his whole past attitude. We had no disagreements with the Bolsheviks, but with the Mensheviks things were going badly . . . Matters reached the point of an almost total break between Trotsky and Martov – whom, by the way, Trotsky always respected as a political intellect – and at the same time a break between all of us Left Internationalists and the Martov group.'[57]

In Paris, says Lunacharsky, Trotsky grew 'greatly in stature in my eyes as a statesman and in the future he grew even more. I do not know whether it was because I knew him better and he was better able to demonstrate the full measure of his powers when working on a grander scale or because in fact the experience of the Revolution and its problems really did mature him and enlarge the sweep of his wings.'[58] Perhaps, as in 1905, Trotsky had a sense of history speeding up, an intimation that events could yet point in the direction of revolution.

Trotsky's anti-war stance was located somewhere between Martov and Lenin. Martov opposed the war on purely pacifist grounds, while Lenin argued it should be converted into an immediate civil war against all bosses and warmongers.[59] The first socialist anti-war conference was held at Zimmerwald in Switzerland. In contrast to the old meetings of the Socialist International, it was a tiny gathering. It is said that the entire conference could have fitted in four stagecoaches.

At Zimmerwald Lenin noted that the French and German socialist parties had supported the war. The old Socialist International had been forever tainted by this betrayal, he said, and he hoped that the anti-war forces would unite and form a new movement, a new International that would resume the struggle for socialism. In the end, however, Trotsky's more conciliatory motion won the day.

In the autumn of 1916 Trotsky was summarily expelled from France. He sent an open letter to Jules Guesde (1845–1922), for many years the representative of French Marxism, but now the French Minister for War. *Is it possible for an honest socialist not to fight against you?* he asked. *In an epoch when bourgeois society – whose mortal enemy you, Jules Guesde, once were – has disclosed its true nature through and through, you have transformed the Socialist Party into a docile chorus accompanying the coryphaei of capitalist banditry . . . Step down, Jules Guesde, from your military automobile, get out of the cage where the capitalist state has shut you up, and look around a little. Perhaps fate will for once, and for the last time, have pity on your sorry old age and you will hear the muted sound of approaching events. We await them; we summon them; we prepare them.*[60]

Trotsky was perhaps even more certain than Lenin of eventual victory.

The Revolution Made (1917)

The longer it rumbled on, the less popular the war became. Millions died in Russia and the rest of Europe. Peasants saw their children taken away. Workers went on strike against the harsh discipline in the factories. Townspeople protested against rationing. Those who had claimed credit for the war in its early days of popularity were transformed in the public mind from heroes to villains. There were protests throughout Europe and Russia was no exception.

In February 1917 a wave of street demonstrations broke out in Petrograd. On International Women's Day (23 February) women took to the streets demanding bread. The following day, 200,000 workers went on strike across the city. In the ensuing street battles the initiative passed from the people to the state and back again. The Tsar's soldiers opened fire on the crowds, but the crowds only grew in number. Revolutionaries were arrested, but more were willing to take their place. On 26 February Nicholas II dissolved parliament, but the Duma voted to continue 'unofficially'. Suddenly the tide was turning. The Cossack military units refused to open fire on the demonstrators and on 28 February the Tsar's ministers were arrested.

Tsar Nicholas II under arrest at Tsarkoe Selo in 1917

'Internal popular disturbances threaten to have a disastrous effect on the future conduct of this persistent war . . . In agreement with the Imperial Duma, We have thought it well to renounce the Throne of the Russian Empire and to lay down the supreme power . . . We direct Our brother to conduct the affairs of State in full and inviolable union with the representatives of the people in the legislative bodies on those principles which will be established by them, and on which He will take an inviolable oath . . . We call on Our faithful sons of the Fatherland to fulfil their sacred duty to the Fatherland, to obey the Tsar in the heavy moment of national trials and to help Him, together with the representatives of the people, to guide the Russian Empire on the road to victory, welfare, and glory.

May the Lord God help Russia!'

NICHOLAS II'S ABDICATION
PROCLAMATION, 2 MARCH 1917

Nicholas II, the last Russian Tsar, abdicated on 15 March 1917 (2 March in the Julian calendar) in favour of his brother the Grand Duke Mikhail (who abdicated the following day!). The Social Revolutionaries and the Mensheviks looked to the liberals to lead the country, for they still maintained Russia had to experience a period of capitalism before socialism could begin.

The new situation was characterized by Trotsky as one of *dual power*. On the one side, a cabinet of ministers emerged that received the support of generals, businessmen and the press. It was an attempt by business leaders to bring order to the crisis, but even as Russia's propertied classes were organizing, so were the workers. On the other side, in the midst of the Revolution, the Soviet was re-established. Its leaders agreed to recognize the cabinet only 'in so far' as it obeyed the Revolution. It was not yet clear which of these two sides would triumph.

Trotsky once again hurried back to Russia, just as he had for the 1905 Revolution. After being deported from France, he had gone to live in America, where he would be remembered as an obscure Brooklyn tailor who somehow became a leading personality in the Russian Revolution.

In April Lenin also returned from exile and both men agreed that a second insurrection was needed and that its success would depend on the growth of the Revolution in the rest of Europe. Each man thought he had converted the other to his way of thinking, Trotsky with perhaps greater justice. He was, after all, the theorist of permanent revolution. Time and again, leading Bolsheviks argued that the Revolution must spread throughout Europe or they would be crushed. 'A great turning-point is at hand,' wrote Lenin. 'We are on the threshold of a world proletarian revolution.'[61] In this changed situation Trotsky's separate, 'inter-regional' organization voted to join the Bolsheviks. Thousands followed him into Lenin's party, including Karl Radek, a socialist journalist with many years experience of revolutionary activity in Poland, Germany and Switzerland; Alexandra Kollontai, the socialist feminist; David Ryazanov (1870–1934), the future head of the Marx-Engels-Institute in Moscow; the Romanian Christian Rakovsky (1873–1941); and V A Antonov-Ovseenko (1884–1938), who led the assault on the Winter Palace.

Born in Poland, Karl Radek (1885–1939?) became a socialist and participated in the 1905 Revolution. A supporter of Trotsky in the 1920s, he later capitulated to Stalin. Caught up in the show trials, he was sentenced to ten year's imprisonment and was never seen again.

In the immediate aftermath of February 1917 the moderate socialists came to the fore. The early leaders of the Petrograd Soviet came from the ranks of the Mensheviks and the Social Revolutionaries, the inheritors of the populist tradition. Personalities such as the Narodnik Victor Chernov had participated in the first and second Dumas after 1905, the 'radical' parliaments that the Tsar had closed down. The reputation of these leaders as dissidents was therefore long established. In addition, their strategy fitted with the will of the cities at that early stage of the Revolution.

The Mensheviks in particular argued that the revolution should be followed by a long period of capitalist stability. One

An early Russian feminist, Alexandra Kollontai (1872–1952) was radicalized after meeting women workers. A Menshevik, then a Bolshevik, she was a commissar in the first Bolshevik left Social Revolutionary government and later supported the Workers' Opposition within the Bolshevik Party. From this platform she attacked bureaucracy and argued for the recreation of the soviet system. Isolated by Stalin, Kollontai accepted a series of junior appointments in the regime and was one of the few old Bolsheviks to survive the purges.

prominent Menshevik, Irakli Tsereteli (1881–1960), wrote: 'It's true that we have all the power and the Government would go if we lifted a finger, but that would mean a disaster for the Revolution.'[62] Most of the people who had overthrown the Tsar had only a hazy conception of the future. They undoubtedly despised the old order and were eager to make a better future, but without a fully worked-out alternative in mind the people of Petrograd looked to books and meetings for instruction.

John Reed (1887–1920) was an American journalist living in Petrograd at the time and his best-selling book *Ten Days that Shook the World* (1919) is an eye-witness account of the Revolution. 'Lectures, debates, speeches,' he reports, 'in theatres, circuses, school-houses, clubs, Soviet meeting-rooms, Union headquarters, barracks . . . Meetings in the trenches, at the Front, in village squares, factories . . . What a marvellous sight to see Putilovsky Zavod (the Putilov factory) pour out its forty thousand to listen to Social Democrats, Socialist Revolutionaries, Anarchists, anybody, whatever they had to say, as long as they would talk!'[63]

Lunacharsky heard Trotsky speak on many occasions in 1917 and described him as 'probably the greatest orator of our age': 'In my time I have heard all the greatest parliamentarians and popular tribunes of socialism and very many famous orators of the bourgeois world and I would find it difficult to name any of them . . . whom I could put in the same class as Trotsky. His impressive

Demonstration of revolutionary democrats in Petrograd 18 June 1917

appearance, his handsome, sweeping gestures, the powerful rhythm of his speech, his loud but never fatiguing voice, the remarkable coherence and literary skill of his phrasing, the richness of imagery, scalding irony, his soaring pathos, his rigid logic, clear as polished steel – those are Trotsky's virtues as a speaker. He can speak in lapidary phrases or throw off a few unusually well-aimed shafts and he can give a magnificent set-piece political speech of the kind that previously I had only heard from Jaurès. I have seen Trotsky speaking for two and a half to three hours in front of a totally silent, standing audience listening as though spellbound to his monumental political treatise. Most of what Trotsky had to say I knew already and naturally every politician often has to repeat the same ideas again and again in front of new crowds, yet every time Trotsky managed to clothe the same thought in a different form.'[64]

Trotsky's favourite venue was the Modern Circus in Petrograd, which attracted a mixed audience of soldiers and women, the dispossessed and dreamers: *I spoke from out of a warm cavern of human bodies; whenever I stretched out my hands I would touch someone, and a grateful movement in response would give me to understand I was not to worry about it, not to break off my speech, but to keep on. No speaker, no matter how exhausted, could resist the electric tension of that impassioned human throng. At times it seemed as if I felt, with my lips, the stern inquisitiveness of this crowd that had become merged with a single whole. Then all the arguments and words thought out in advance would break and recede under the imperative pressure of sympathy, and other words, other arguments, utterly unexpected by the orator but needed by these people, would emerge in full array from my subconsciousness. On such occasions I felt as if I were listening to the speaker from outside, trying to keep pace with his ideas, afraid that, like a somnambulist, he might fall off the edge of the roof at the sound of my conscious meaning.*[65]

With his supreme talents as an orator Trotsky became the public face of Bolshevism. However, the problem now was how to take the Revolution forwards. In July huge demonstrations demanded the removal of all ministers and their replacement by a socialist government. Tens of thousands of workers marched from the great industrial plants such as Putilov. The sailors of Kronstadt also demanded a second revolution. The Bolsheviks attempted to hold back this wave of the uprising, arguing that although Petrograd was ready the other Russian cities were not yet convinced. On 4 July some 500,000 people assembled on the streets of Petrograd. Their demands were simple: the Social Revolutionaries, the Mensheviks and the Bolsheviks should form an all-socialist government. In the absence of any clear strategy for seizing power, the uprising was defeated. The tide began to turn and there were rumours that the Bolsheviks were in the pay of Germany. Lenin was forced into hiding and Trotsky was arrested.

July was the toughest month. Special courts were established to try the leaders of the left and several reactionaries came to taunt Trotsky in his cell. On one occasion, a right-wing officer and patriot mocked him openly while Trotsky's young sons were in the room. The oldest boy dashed at the officer with a chair, the youngest with a table knife. They were restrained by the grown-ups and left the room sobbing hysterically. Trotsky's daughters were also with him. They had attended his meetings at the Modern Circus and had also taken part in the July uprising. One of them had lost her glasses in the jostling crowds and they worried now that they might also lose their father, who had only recently re-entered their lives.

Meanwhile, the Soviet continued to meet and other workers' councils were established in the smaller cities, as well as soviets of peasants, soldiers and sailors. The movement had been weakened, but was far from finished. It was in this context that the new prime minister of the Provisional Government, a former populist called Alexander Kerensky, began to plot the final defeat of the Revolution. He saw the country torn by deep divisions and felt that only his brand of strong leadership could heal the wounds. The war effort would have to continue. Russian factories had to reopen. In fact, a

Alexander Kerensky the first Premier of the Russian Republic photographed in Stuttgart 1951

Born, like Lenin, in Simbirsk to an aristocratic family, Alexander Kerensky (1881–1970) became a radical lawyer. He joined the Social Revolutionaries and through them was elected to parliament as a Trudovik (or 'Labourite'). He was vice-chair of the Petrograd Soviet, but used this position to advance his own career. Kerensky led the Provisional Government, fleeing Petrograd when the October Revolution broke out.

counter-revolutionary dictatorship was required. Kerensky's commander-in-chief, General Lavr Kornilov (1870–1918) was of a similar opinion. Indeed, Kornilov began making military preparations for a coup. In his view Lenin should be hanged and the Soviet dispersed.

In the end it was the so-called Kornilov affair that enabled the Bolsheviks to regroup after the failure of the July putsch. When General Kornilov began to threaten the prime minister's hold on power, Kerensky decided to throw in his lot with the lesser of two evils and petitioned the Soviet for aid.

Trotsky and the Bolsheviks were released and General Kornilov's conspiracy was undermined by the work of sympathetic railwaymen, who shunted his troops the wrong way along the sidings. Many of Kornilov's troops were Muslims from the south and agitators went among them asking how far they trusted this reactionary general to support their national or religious rights?

Meanwhile, the Bolsheviks faced their own dilemma. Should they ally with Kerensky, knowing that he had jailed them once and would do so again, or should they stand alone? Trotsky later explained how this complex issue was resolved: *On August 26 (old style) 1917 General Kornilov led his Cossack corps and one irregular division against Petrograd. At the helm of power stood Kerensky, lackey of the bourgeoisie and three-quarters a confederate of Kornilov. Lenin was still in hiding because of the accusation that he was in the service of the Hohenzollerns* [the Germans]. *For the same accusation, I was at that time incarcerated in solitary confinement in Kresty Prison.*

How did the Bolsheviks proceed in this question? They also had a right to say: 'In order to defeat the Korniloviad — we must first defeat the Kerenskiad.' They said this more than once, for it was correct and necessary for all the subsequent propaganda. But that was entirely inadequate for offering resistance to Kornilov on August 26 and on the days that followed, and for preventing him from butchering the Petrograd proletariat. That is why the Bolsheviks did not content them-selves with a general appeal to the workers and soldiers to break with the conciliators and to support the red united front of the Bolsheviks. No, the Bolsheviks proposed the united front struggle to the Mensheviks and the Social Revolutionaries and created together with them joint organizations of struggle.[66]

'. . . the Kornilov affair . . . resulted from a struggle in Kerensky's mind between his sense that as the head of State in a situation of near-anarchy and a looming German offensive he needed the army's support, and his fear as a socialist intellectual that the army was likely to breed a counter-revolutionary Napoleon. In private conversation . . . Kerensky conceded that his actions at the time had been strongly influenced by the experi-ence of the French Revolution.'

Soon after General Kornilov's defeat, the Bolsheviks won majorities in soviet after soviet. As their star rose, the question began to be asked: how to defeat Kerensky? From exile, Lenin sent letters to his comrades begging them to act. 'Events are prescrib-ing our task so clearly for us that procrastination is becoming pos-itively *criminal*,' he wrote on 1 October. 'In Germany the begin-ning of a revolution is obvious . . . The elections in Moscow – 47 per cent Bolsheviks – are a tremendous victory. Together with the Left Social Revolutionaries we have an *obvious* majority *in the coun-try*.' Everything, Lenin was convinced, was pushing the Bolsheviks towards victory. 'To "wait" would be a crime to the Revolution.'[67]

But the Bolshevik Central Committee delayed making a deci-sion. Finally, on 23 October 1917, the vote was taken. Two voices were decisive: Lenin's, arguing for immediate action, and Trotsky's, outlining the precise details of such action. Trotsky maintained that the offensive should take place under the aegis of the All-Russian Congress of Soviets, which was due to sit at the end of the month. In the post-revolutionary period, he argued, the future should belong to the Soviet. In justifying the insurrection, it was important to point out the preparations that Kerensky was making to crush the council. Russia was approaching a final showdown. Only one force could triumph: the Provisional Government or the Soviet. The very defence of the Soviet required a successful uprising.

This speech was only one of Trotsky's many contributions to the events of 1917, but it was among his most important. Lenin could sense the desire of the masses for change; he felt it and angrily expressed it. But he was less interested in the question of which banner to fight under. To Trotsky, however, it was everything and his argument made tactical sense. If the Bolsheviks had carried through a revolution in their own name, without the backing of greater numbers, they would have met hostility much earlier on and the Revolution might have been lost. He also had a better understanding of why revolution was needed: to change society in order that particular institutions of workers' power (the soviets) could rule. He was not prepared to defer such principles until after the dust had settled.

A supporter of Lenin's from 1903, Grigori Zinoviev (1883–1936) joined the leading circles of Bolshevism in 1907 and rarely fell out of prominence thereafter. Together with Kamenev, he attempted to halt the October Revolution. He allied successfully with Stalin against Trotsky in 1923–4, then unsuccessfully with Trotsky against Stalin in 1925. Zinoviev perished following the first Moscow show trial.

In the last days of October, two men spoke out against the rising: Grigori Zinoviev and Lev Kamenev. They even published the secret date on which the insurrection was planned. A furious Lenin called them 'strike-breakers', but they remained in the party. So paralysed was the

The successors to Lenin: Stalin with his colleagues and future victims Rykov, Kamenev and Zinoviev

old Provisional Government, however, that it could not even act on a direct warning.

In the end the Revolution took place under the aegis of the Military Revolutionary Committee (MRC) of the Petrograd Soviet, one of the joint bodies whose influence went back to the struggle against General Kornilov. It began when the MRC sent troops to arrest Kerensky's ministers. The Winter Palace was stormed and Kerensky fled. As President of the Soviet, Trotsky was in charge. Even years later, he could only describe this moment in the present tense, the events were still so vivid. When he sent instructions for the MRC to advance on the Palace, he admits *I do not yet believe in the force of my order. The Revolution is still too trusting, too generous, too optimistic and light-hearted. It prefers to threaten with arms rather than really use them.*[68]

Lev Kamenev (1883–1936), Trotsky's brother-in-law, edited the Bolshevik paper *Proletary* and led the RSDLP faction in the 1914 Duma. He allied with Zinoviev in the 1920s. He, too, was a victim of the first show trial.

He waited. *All is well. It could not have gone much better. Now I may leave the telephone. I sit down on the couch. The nervous tension lessons. A dull sense of fatigue comes over me. 'Give me a cigarette,' I say to Kamenev. (In those years I still smoked, but only spasmodically.) I take one or two puffs, but suddenly with the words, 'Only this was lacking!' I faint . . . As I come to, I see Kamenev's frightened face bending over me. 'Shall I get some medicine?' he asks. 'It would be much better,' I answer after a moment's reflection, 'if you got me something to eat.' I try to remember when I last had food, but I can't. At all events it was not yesterday.*[69]

The All-Russian Congress of Soviets voted to support the uprising and a new coalition was announced of Bolsheviks and left-wing Social Revolutionaries. A presidium was elected to head the Soviet, composed of fourteen Bolsheviks, seven Social Revolutionaries, three Mensheviks and one member of the faction around the novelist Maxim Gorky. Trotsky's old mentor Julius Martov protested that 'This is not the moment to seize power,' but his concerns were swept aside and Martov's faction walked out. When Trotsky spoke, John Reed reports, he was borne to the platform on a wave of applause 'that burst into cheers and a rising house, thunderous'.[70]

Our rising has been victorious, Trotsky shouted to Martov. *Now they tell us: Renounce your victory, yield, make a compromise. With whom? With whom, I am asking, shall we make this compromise? With these miserable little groups that have left or with those that make these proposals . . . You are bankrupt. You have played out your role. Go where you belong: to the dustheap of history!*[71]

For days afterwards the situation remained unclear. The Bolsheviks were accused of killing several of Kerensky's ministers. In fact, one person had died. The battleship *Aurora*, with which

As the first commissar for public welfare in the Bolshevik government Alexandra Kollontai greatly improved the status of women, a photograph from 1910

Trotsky had 'bombarded' the Winter Palace, had been firing blanks. The Bolsheviks were also rumoured to stand for one-party rule and groups of anxious Social Revolutionaries and Mensheviks debated whether or not to lend them support.

According to Reed, the decisive moment came when Lenin returned to appear before the All-Russian Congress of Soviets on 26 October. He put forward a resolution 'To the Peoples and Governments of all the Belligerent Nations'. The new government's proposal of immediate, public negotiations for peace won considerable support. The Ukrainian socialists, the Lithuanians, the Poles, the Latvians, the Social Revolutionaries and

'It was just 8.40 when a thundering wave of cheers announced the entrance of the presidium, with Lenin – great Lenin – among them. A short, stocky figure, with a big head set down in his shoulders, bald and bulging. Little eyes, a snubbish nose, wide, generous mouth, and heavy chin; clean-shaven now, but already beginning to bristle with the well-known beard of his past and future. Dressed in shabby clothes, his trousers much too long for him. Unimpressive, to be the idol of a mob, loved and revered as perhaps few leaders in history have been. A strange popular leader – a leader purely by virtue of intellect; colourless, humourless, uncompromising and detached, without picturesque idiosyncrasies – but with the power of explaining profound ideas in simple terms, of analysing a concrete situation. And combined with shrewdness, the greatest intellectual audacity.'

FROM JOHN REED'S
Ten Days That Shook the World

Mensheviks all supported it. 'Something was kindled in these men', writes Reed. 'One spoke of the "coming World Revolution of which we are the advance guard"; another of "the new age of brotherhood when all the peoples will become one great family".' Lenin's motion was passed unanimously. 'Suddenly, by common impulse, we found ourselves on our feet, mumbling together into the smooth lifting unison of the *Internationale*. A grizzled old soldier was sobbing like a child. Alexandra Kollontai rapidly winked the tears back. The immense sound rolled through the hall, burst windows and doors and soared into the sky. "The war is ended! The war is ended!" said a young workman near me, his face shining.'[72] Only now did the actuality of the Revolution strike home.

Reflecting on this period of his life, Trotsky gave full credit to Lenin for inspiring and directing the revolt. Many others had played a part, but without the fierce determination of Lenin the Bolsheviks would not have seized power at that decisive moment. *Had we not taken power in October*, said Trotsky, *we would never have taken it. Our strength on the eve of October lay in the fact that the masses were pouring*

*into our party because they believed that it would do what others had
failed. If the masses had detected in us the slightest sign of vacillation,
of the desire to wait, or of a divergence between our words and our
deeds, within two or three months the tide would have ebbed away just
as it ebbed away from the SRs and the Mensheviks. The bourgeoisie
would have obtained a respite . . . the proletarian revolution would
have been postponed indefinitely. Lenin understood and sensed this;
hence his anxiety and fear, his distrust and the frantic pressure, which
saved the Revolution.*[73]

The first six months after October were the halcyon days of
the Russian Revolution. The workers occupied the factories;
domestic labour was abolished; peasants were encouraged to take
ownership of the land; and a vigorous workers' democracy flourished alongside the relative liberation of women and the creativity of radical artists. The authority of the head of the family was
abolished and marriage became a purely civil process; women had
the vote for the first time and discrimination against illegitimate
children was ended. It was an extraordinary flurry of legislation.
In 1917 women had the vote in no other countries apart from
Norway and Denmark, while free abortion was available nowhere
else in the world except Russia. There remained considerable
obstacles to progress, however. Not all of the laws were fully
implemented, and how many women in the rural areas had any
access to the reforms that were passed in their name?

In the winter of 1917–18 the new Bolshevik–Social
Revolutionary government agreed to hold elections for a
Constituent Assembly. Afterwards, the coalition could only claim
to have won a third of the votes. The results were misleading. The
largest single bloc of representatives belonged to the Social
Revolutionaries, yet that party was disintegrating with both its
left and right in turmoil. In the cities most SRs supported the
Soviet government. Their delegates supported the left. In the
countryside, the SRs equivocated. Their representatives opposed

The nephew of a chemist implicated in the assassination of Alexander II, Victor Serge (1880–1947) lived in Belgium and then France, where he was imprisoned for supporting an anarchist gang. He travelled to Russia on the outbreak of the October Revolution. Persuaded of its success, he ceased to support anarchism and came over to the Bolsheviks. Yet Serge never lost his libertarian instincts. He sided with Trotsky against Stalin, suffering a long period of imprisonment and exile as a result. On escaping from Russia he translated Trotsky's works into French, but later broke with him. Serge's *Memoirs of a Revolutionary* (1945) is one of the outstanding documents of this period.

the Revolution. The Assembly was dissolved.

The soviets continued to flourish, however, and while they did the regime retained popular legitimacy. For many months the factory committees had procured fuel and raw materials and supervised the processes of production. By spring 1918 most committees had taken control of every aspect of decision-making, running meetings, accounts and order books.[74] Western parliamentary democracy rests commonly on a division between politics and economics, in which only the former is subject to scrutiny. Economic conditions rest beyond the scope of parliaments, let alone voters. The soviets threatened to break that division for good. Where they flourished, there was a self-governing system of economic democracy that transcended anything then known.

The death penalty was abolished on the morning after the Revolution, although events conspired to undermine this virtuous gesture. The French journalist and radical Victor Serge described one such incident in November 1917 when representatives of the MRC were sent to dissolve a gathering of officers. The Committee took the leaders' guns, but allowed them to go free. 'Foolish clemency,' observed Serge. 'These very Junkers . . . dispersed themselves throughout the length and breadth of Russia and there organized the civil war. The Revolution was to meet them again, at Iaroslav, on the Don, at Kazan, in the Crimea, in Siberia and in every conspiracy nearer home.'[75]

Trotsky and Lenin hoped that their insurrection would be copied in France and Germany. 'We are far from having completed even the transitional period from capitalism to socialism,' wrote Lenin in January 1918. 'We have never cherished the hope that we could finish it without the aid of the international proletariat. We have never had any illusions on that score . . . The final victory of socialism in one country is of course impossible.'[76] Hopes remained high. In the summer of 1917 French soldiers had mutinied against their generals and there was every chance German troops would refuse to fight against Russia. Nevertheless, the Great War rumbled on.

The Sword (1917–1921)

Following the October Revolution sovereignty was transferred into the hands of the All-Russian Soviet, yet this body could only meet infrequently. Between meetings, decisions were taken by a council of people's commissars. From day to day the Bolsheviks ruled in coalition with the left-wing Social Revolutionaries.

Trotsky was given responsibility for managing foreign affairs. All that would be needed, he thought, would be to issue a few revolutionary proclamations and then he could shut up shop. But actually governing proved much harder. For one thing, the old Tsarist civil servants refused to serve under the new government. When Trotsky walked into the ministry to begin work, he found that only the security guards and a few secretaries remained. Meanwhile, Germany proved unwilling to accept the Soviet offer of peace.

At the end of November 1917 Trotsky and a few colleagues arrived at Brest-Litovsk near the Polish border to begin the final peace negotiations. The generals, princes and politicians of the Habsburg and Imperial German empires turned out in force. Trotsky's delegation fraternized with its German equivalent (not the officers, but the ordinary troops) and distributed socialist leaflets.

Trotsky insisted that the discussions between the leaders should be broadcast on the wireless so that ordinary Germans could hear. It was pure theatre and he was determined to signal the difference between the old Russia and the new. He also needed to bargain for time. The German army had already won a decisive military victory and Imperial troops controlled lands as far east as Latvia. Trotsky hoped to negotiate a return to Russia's pre-war borders, but the regions to the west of old Russia were the grain-basket of the nation and such lands as the Ukraine and Russian Poland also contained the most advanced industries. Their loss

Trotsky and the Soviet delegation arrive at Brest-Litovsk to begin final peace negotiations November 1917

could not be accepted easily. Furthermore, the Germans were already in possession and had no interest in conceding land they had already conquered. The only hope, Trotsky saw, was to delay. The longer the negotiations lasted, the more likely it was that Germany would send troops west to fight France, Britain and the United States. Also, more optimistically, the longer a ceasefire remained in force, the greater the chance of a workers' revolution in Germany.

By the spring of 1918 peace negotiations had broken down and the German advance resumed. In one of his accounts Trotsky recalls the fears that began to assail the Bolsheviks. The Communist 'left', led by such men as Bukharin, argued that the new state could sign no treaties, especially not at gunpoint. As long as the Soviets held out, they set an example to the rest of the world and brought closer the day of the German revolution and eventual peace. The answer to the German attack was to declare a revolutionary war. Bolsheviks on the right, however, dismissed such talk as utopian. The Revolution had only come to power by promising the people peace. What slogan was better known among the masses than the promise of 'Bread, Peace, Land'? The Russians had no appetite for war, so peace should be concluded on any terms. What would happen if the Germans marched on Moscow?

Then we shall withdraw further east, towards the Urals (Lenin replied). The Kuznets Basin is rich in coal. We shall set up an Uralo-Kuznets Republic based on the regional industry and the coal of Kuznets and supported by the proletariat of the Urals and by as many workers as we shall be able to bring with us from Moscow and Petrograd. We shall hold out. If we have to, we shall retreat even further, beyond the Urals. We will go even to Kamchatka, but we shall hold out. The international balances of forces will change a dozen times, and from our Republic in the Urals and Kuznets, we will return to Moscow and Petrograd . . .

Lenin was not joking, continues Trotsky. *True to himself, he analysed the situation through to the end, to its worst possibilities. The concept of the Uralo-Kuznets Republic was necessary to him in order to strengthen the own conviction that all was not yet lost, and that there was and could not be any room for a strategy of despair.*[77]

Soon afterwards the two men swapped sides in the debate. Trotsky continued to argue for stalling tactics, while Lenin was persuaded of the need for pragmatism. In the end the Germans continued to march eastwards and the Bolsheviks only prevented further annexations by signing a wretched peace treaty.

The Treaty of Brest-Litovsk marked the turning point at which the new government lost control of its future. Far from solving their problems it marked the start of another civil war. The left Social Revolutionaries were already looking for an excuse to leave the government and now they complained that the Bolsheviks should never have signed such a humiliating peace deal. With their roots in the populist tradition, the language of nationalism came easier to the SRs and they left the coalition on 'nationalist' grounds, encouraging their supporters to revolt. Two thousand men, armed with field guns and machine guns, captured the Bolshevik commissar Felix Dzerzhinsky (1877–1926) and opened fire on the Kremlin.

Other forces used this rift at the top of Soviet society to start their own revolts. Turkish troops invaded the Transcaucasus and German armies advanced into the Ukraine. American, French, Japanese, British and Czech troops invaded. The French occupied Odessa. There were 50,000 foreign soldiers on Russian soil.

This outside intervention only succeeded in stirring up local elements. Kaledin organized an anti-Soviet army from the Don. Armenians and Azerbaijanis demanded their independence. Each of the established Russian parties, from the Monarchists to the Mensheviks, was now ranged in a 'White' coalition against the Soviet regime. The old Menshevik Georgi Plekhanov spoke for the moderates, calling the Bolsheviks 'imbeciles, traitors, provocateurs . . . We must not only master but crush this vermin, drown it in blood. This is the price of Russia's safety.'[78] Such sentiments were commonplace and hundreds of thousands of Russians would die in the civil war.

Terror was largely the creation of the anti-Bolshevik Whites. In Finland alone, the Whites killed between 10,000 and 20,000 people. In the Ukraine whole towns of Jews followed the Red frontline, advancing and retreating with it and fleeing their opponents, because those who remained at home risked death from White pogroms. *The more ferocious and dangerous is the resistance of the class enemy who has been overthrown*, Trotsky had written, *the more inevitably does the system of repression take the form of a system of terror.*[79]

For the first time, in the spring of 1918, the Bolsheviks

Trotsky the creator of the Red Army at the Front 1918

began to use violence against their domestic opponents. They established an All-Russian Extraordinary Commission to Fight Counter-Revolution and Sabotage or 'Cheka' (a forerunner of the KGB). A veteran of many Tsarist prisons, Dzerzhinsky was placed in charge under joint Bolshevik SR control. At first the secret police of the Cheka refrained from systematic violence. Between January and June 1918 it authorized 22 death sentences, mostly of a 'non-political' character. But in conditions of civil war the power of the Cheka grew rapidly. To secure the Revolution's future, Trotsky authorized the use of 'Red terror' against the Whites. Both sides killed tens of thousands. Meanwhile the links between town and countryside were destroyed: no bread got through to feed Moscow or Petrograd and millions more died from starvation and disease.

Charged with organizing a Red Army to defend the Revolution, Trotsky created a fighting force of millions around a cadre of working-class Bolsheviks from the factories. Once again he spoke before the Petrograd Soviet, demanding volunteers. It was the most heroic period of his life and a time of frenetic organization.[80] Trotsky became quite another person according to his supporter, Karl Radek, who noted that 'The Revolution changed to a sword the pen of its best publicist.'[81] The Red Army fought on a front more than 5,000 miles long. White armies thrust deep into the interior, but the Reds fought back.

Travelling everywhere in a special train, Trotsky's mere appearance could halt or even reverse headlong retreat. *We always had in reserve a few zealous communists to fill in the breaches*, he later recalled, *a hundred or so good fighting men, a small stock of boots, leather jackets, medicaments, machine-guns, field-glasses, maps, watches and all sorts of gifts. Of course, the actual material resources of the train were slight in comparison with the needs of the army. But they were constantly being replenished . . . Without constant changes and improvisations, the war would have been utterly impossible for us. The train initiated those, and at the same time regulated them. If we have an impulse of initiative to the front and its immediate rear, we took care to direct it into the channels of the general system. I do not want to say that we always succeeded in this. But . . . we did achieve the principal thing – victory.*[82]

In October 1918 Petrograd was under threat: White troops had reached the outskirts of the city. Trotsky took charge of the capital's defence. Ersatz tanks were built in a matter of days, while canals, walls and fences were fortified. Trotsky moved constantly from meeting to barricade to assembly line until the southern half of Petrograd was converted into a giant fortress. *A new spirit was breathing from the workers' districts to the barracks, the rear units, and even to the army in the field.*[83] The period of retreat was turned into one of advance and a week later Trotsky appeared before the Soviet executive in Moscow to report victory.[84]

Even then, however, there was room in his life for something other than politics. He and Natalia proudly watched their growing sons approaching adulthood and in the very midst of the civil war he was reunited with his elderly father. *The October Revolution found my father a very prosperous man,* Trotsky recalled. *My mother had died in 1910, but my father lived to see the rule of the Soviets. At the height of the civil war, which raged with especial fury in the South and was accompanied by constant changes of government, the old man of seventy was obliged to walk hundreds of miles to find shelter in Odessa. The Reds were a menace to him because he was rich; the Whites persecuted him because he was my father. After the South had been freed of White soldiers by the Soviet troops, he was able to come to Moscow. He had lost all his savings in the Revolution. For more than a year he ran a small state mill near Moscow. The Commissar of Food at that time, Tzurupa, used to enjoy chatting with him on agricultural subjects. My father died of typhus in the spring of 1922, at the every moment when I was reading my report at the Fourth Congress of the Communist International.* [85]

By the spring of 1920 it seemed as if the Soviet regime might yet survive. The left-wing American reporter Louise Bryant (1885–1936) dispatched a vivid account of the man: 'In Trotsky we discern something distinctly elemental. He looks like a fighter, with his burning eyes and sharp decisive way of speaking, his gestures, his quick regular gait. When he is calm he does not appear to be himself. But even in ordinary conversation he bestirs himself, he throws himself headlong into every discussion, and the listener is so carried away that he remembers it all afterward with astonishment.' [86]

Under Trotsky's leadership, Bryant reported, the Red Army recruited the young and the talented, even at times the children of the bourgeoisie: 'As the White Generals went down to defeat one after the other, the young men even of conservative parents came to believe that if they could not swallow the Communist formulas whole, they could, at least, remain loyal Russians. And once in the military schools, they fell under the influence of revolutionary soldiers. Being young and full of Slavic idealism, they often capitulated and in such cases were rapidly promoted.' [87] The soldiers were urged to attend art galleries and theatres, while art exhibitions and lectures took place in the soldiers' clubs. They acted in their own plays, mostly on the theme of the Revolution. As for Trotsky, Bryant concluded, 'One can make vast speculation . . . He is the sort of man who, if he is given full power in a great plan of this kind, will work miracles, but if he is hampered by petty labour disputes and a thousand petty jealousies, will fail utterly.' [88]

As the Red cities defied capture, so the opportunity remained for the world's workers to rescue the Revolution. The gamble of 1917 might yet have paid off. A sailors' uprising brought an end to Kaiser Wilhelm II, Germany's last Kaiser, and with him removed the First World War was over. Lenin and Trotsky launched the Communist or 'Third' International in 1919 as a means to unite the various parties who had opposed war and to spread the Russian Revolution. Soviet governments were established in Hungary and Bavaria.

Trotsky and his son Leon Sedov at a review of the Red Army

At the start of 1919 a second insurrection began in Berlin. It was supported by the rank and file of the German Spartacists (later the Communist Party) and by many Independent Socialists, but by almost none of the governing Socialist Party. The revolt failed and rather than pursue transformation, the leading German socialists were more determined to arm former officers to fight against the left. The leaders of German Communism – Rosa Luxemburg and Karl Liebknecht (1871–1919) – were murdered. For the next four years Germany remained in crisis. Large numbers of workers continued to strike, but the chance of immediate success had already been lost.

Throughout Europe and the world there were areas where the Russian Revolution possessed enormous reserves of goodwill. Even in Britain, when Lloyd George's coalition govern-

Kaiser Wilhelm II (1859–1941) became Emperor of Germany in 1888 following the death of Frederick II. After the assassination of Archduke Franz Ferdinand of Austria-Hungary by a Serb nationalist on 28 June 1914, Wilhelm encouraged Austria-Hungary to revenge itself on Serbia, little realizing that an attack on Serbia would bring France, Russia and Britain into what became the First World War. With revolution spreading to Berlin, Wilhelm was forced to abdicate on 9 November 1918. He lived in exile in Holland and, following the Armistice, escaped extradition as a war criminal. Later he was a keen supporter of Adolf Hitler (1889–1945).

ment tried to wage open war against the Soviets, the left organized a huge 'Hands off Russia' campaign. British dockers and sailors mutinied rather than assist the army in making preparations for war. The Russian Revolution was praised, above all, for having brought an end to the war and the British people were broadly sympathetic towards it, although the majority held back from active solidarity. When a British Communist Party was formed in 1920 it had just 6,000 members. Few workers' leaders properly understood the revolutionary idealism of the new Russia and Bolshevism remained a minority movement in Britain and elsewhere.

In Russia, meanwhile, the goals of the Revolution were being distorted by a bloody civil war. When factory workers left home to fight the White armies, the soviets fell apart. In many places they continued to meet, but they lacked their former authority. In fact, the most important democratic advances of the first few months of the Revolution were lost in a bloody struggle for survival. When conscription was resumed, the production of industrial goods dried up. With the Bolshevik cadres fighting elsewhere, one-man management was introduced in the factories. Bread was scarce and grain was taken by force from the peasants. The Bolsheviks survived all of this, but at a terrible cost.

As the civil war continued, leading Bolsheviks debated the

future. Earlier than anyone else, Trotsky realized that the system of War Communism was unsustainable, though he vacillated between two alternative futures. One possibility was to end the system of grain requisitions and to return to something like the economic order that had existed before October 1917. This was the most peaceful option and it was what many ordinary Russians wanted, but was it a socialist solution? The other alternative was to build on the success of the Red Army and use it as the basis on which to found a new society. A modern Russia could be built through a centralized system of industrial organization. After some hesitation, he opted for the latter.

Trotsky defended his conduct during this period in *Terrorism and Communism* (1920), a withering attack on Karl Kautsky and on the whole tradition of Western parliamentary socialism. Writing towards the end of the civil war, he confidently announces that reformism has lost and that the Bolsheviks have won a decisive victory over their opponents. He also defends the dissolution of the Constituent Assembly, arguing that the soviets were more democratic. This argument might have held water in 1917, but it was less true in 1920, by which time the local soviets had been absorbed by the state. Trotsky went on to argue that the success of the Red Army had been achieved through

Founded at a meeting attended by 35 delegates from large parties in Russia, Norway, Germany and smaller groups in 17 other countries, the Communist International (or Comintern) was designed as a revolutionary centre bringing together the experience of parties committed to profound social change. It was dubbed the Third International to distinguish it from that of Marx's day and from the Second (Socialist) International. The strategy of establishing the Comintern derived from Lenin and Trotsky's insistence on the need for further revolutions in order to secure the survival of the new Soviet state. As the leaders of the Soviet Union were won over to the rival doctrine of 'socialism in one country', the purpose of the Comintern became less obvious and it was dissolved by Stalin in 1943.

a process of planning and central direction, epitomized by military conscription. The system had proved itself in war – why not continue it in peacetime?

Trotsky also advocates using forced labour to rebuild Russia: *We . . . oppose capitalist slavery by socially regulated labour on the basis of an economic plan, obligatory for the whole people and consequently compulsory for each worker in the country. Without this, we cannot even dream of a transition to socialism. The element of material, physical, compulsion may be greater or less; that depends on many conditions, on the degree of wealth or poverty in the country, on the heritage of the past, on the general level of culture, on the condition of transport, on the administrative apparatus, etc., etc. But obligation and, consequently, compulsion, are essential conditions in order to bind down the bourgeois anarchy, to secure socialization of the means of production and to reconstruct economic life on the basis of a single plan.*[89]

He outlines a general system of industrial conscription, whereby people's working lives could be directed by a single plan – and this idea was of crucial importance. At the heart of Marxism is the claim that our social relationships shape all other aspects of our lives, the most important being those of the workplace. Where people are allowed to become the mere subjects of a single commander, the chances of them scrutinizing their leader are practically non-existent. In other words, industrial conscription is incompatible with democracy or socialism.[90]

We can make excuses for Trotsky. After all, the working class had been decimated in the civil war and Russia was starving. In this context he was not the only socialist to lose all sense of proportion. Other leading Communists (including Bukharin) even welcomed Russia's rampant inflation on the grounds that it would facilitate the rapid abolition of money. Such a view might appear comic today, although Trotsky's ideas at this time are far less amusing. Significantly, he made no attempt to justify them in his memoirs.

Trotsky's biographer Isaac Deutscher has called this moment

'defeat in victory'. The creation of the Red Army had enabled the Bolsheviks to win the civil war, but this victory had resulted in the destruction of the Russian working class. The settled work-force in the factories had been broken up and the best socialists sent into battle. Now how was the state supposed to feed the returning workers? The application of a market economy might conceivably help increase production in both town and country, but for obvious reasons most leading Bolsheviks drew back from this option: surely they had fought to abolish capitalism?

Another possibility was state intervention and Trotsky was not alone in arguing that the state should shoulder the burden of rebuilding Russian industry. Few Bolsheviks opposed his proposals, yet in going along this path there was always the risk that the inequality of the workers might become acceptable in the future. In a speech in 1920, Trotsky argued that old-fashioned serf labour had in its time been a *progressive phenomenon*.[91]

It might be possible to defend this argument on the grounds that feudalism had created a more democratic and equal society than the slave societies that preceded it, but Trotsky's point was not historical; he was more concerned with the present. He appears to accept a situation in which workers' rights are deferred indefinitely. 'Carried away by his desire to justify the measures he sponsored,' writes Deutscher, 'he . . . came very near to talking like an apologist for past systems of coercion and exploitation.' [92]

In March 1921 Trotsky defended the existing democracy of the times against criticisms made by the Workers' Opposition and others. The words he used were uncharacteristically vague. *The Party is obliged to maintain its dictatorship, regardless of wavering in the spontaneous moods of the masses, regardless of the temporary vacillations even in the working class. The awareness is for us the indispensable unifying element. The dictatorship does not base itself at every given moment on the formal principle of a workers' democracy, although the workers' democracy is, of course, the only method by which the masses can be drawn more and more into polit-*

ical life.[93] Elsewhere, Trotsky spoke of *the revolutionary birthright of the Party.*[94] He seemed to be saying that the Bolsheviks' Marxist principles allowed them to represent the workers, even though the workers themselves were hostile. But wasn't the first principle of Marxism the idea of working-class self-emancipation?

There seem to have been two different conceptions of socialism fighting for control of Trotsky's mind. One was the modest claim that the party should simply hold on to power and hope that the Revolution would spread internationally. The Russian working class had been atomized and it was now meaningless to advocate a return to a workers' democracy (although this notion hinted at the direction Trotsky's Marxism would take in later decades). The second choice was to argue that the party had a mission to rule, even in the absence of democracy. This idea pointed towards the 'Marxism' of Stalin and the gulags.

It would take the intervention of Lenin and the creation of a different economic order after 1921 to divert Trotsky from the hardline course on which he was now set.

Trotsky leads an inspection of troops on Red Square 1920

The Pockmarked Rival (1921–1922)

What did Trotsky want from 1917? Lunacharsky answered a common criticism. 'It is usual to say of Trotsky that he is ambitious. This is, of course, utter nonsense. I remember Trotsky making a very significant remark in connection with Chernov's acceptance of a ministerial portfolio: *What despicable ambition – to abandon one's place in history in exchange for the untimely offer of a ministerial post.* In that, I think, lay all of Trotsky. There is not a drop of vanity in him, he is totally indifferent to any title or to the trappings of power; he is, however, boundlessly jealous of his own role in history and in that sense he is ambitious. Here he is I think as sincere as he is in his natural love of power.'[95]

Like many of his contemporaries Trotsky had suffered many years of imprisonment and exile for his beliefs. He was not looking for self-advancement. As a young man, he had joined the revolutionary camp in a spirit of altruism. His ideas were those of the socialist left. The point of change was to create a just and equal society that would allow the free development of all people, liberated from the burden of degrading work and the barriers of squalor and hunger.

The Russian Marxists believed that human freedom could not be established without equality, or equality without freedom. In Trotsky's words, *The Revolution is, in the first place, an*

Victor Chernov (1873–1952) studied law at Moscow University where he became the leader of an illegal students' union. A founding member of the Social-Revolutionary Party, he was imprisoned for his views for several years. After living in exile, he returned to Russia during the 1905 Revolution and served in the Provisional Government as Minister of Agriculture. Chernov left Russia and lived in Czechoslovakia before moving to the United States, where he died.

awakening of human personality in the masses, which were supposed to possess no personality. In spite of occasional cruelty and the sanguinary restlessness of its methods, the Revolution is before and above all the awakening of humanity, its onward march, and is marked with a growing respect for the personal dignity of every individual, with an ever increasing concern for those who are weak.[96] Such rhetoric might appear rather abstract today. Too often politicians have abused such phrases as 'the dignity of the weak'. But in order to understand the revolt of the various Russian dissidents against Stalin, we must take such sentiments seriously. Trotsky did not choose to be a revolutionary out of any selfish motives. His ideal of a socialist democracy was heartfelt and genuine.

But Trotsky's opportunity to create the world he wanted to live in was limited by hostile external conditions. Within a year of

Trotsky, Lenin and Kamenev at the 2nd Congress of the Communist International in Petrograd 1920

the Revolution the Russian people had no appetite for further changes. By the winter of 1920–1, few of the militant workers of 1917 were alive. Fewer still had any connection to the trade union movements or the workplaces in which they had previously organized. The majority of Russians were indifferent to the Bolsheviks or outwardly antagonistic. Even after the civil war ended in 1920–1, the Bolsheviks still had to endure widespread peasant revolts. And then came the uprising of the Kronstadt sailors; probably the most important protest faced by Russia's new leaders.

The Kronstadt garrison rose up against Communist rule in the spring of 1920. They argued for the return of the workplace soviets, provided they were purged of all Bolsheviks. It was a significant military revolt. The ice around Kronstadt was melting and very soon the sailors would set a course for Petrograd. Lenin and Trotsky saw little option but to respond by sending troops. One witness, the libertarian Bolshevik Victor Serge, sympathized with the sailors. The real culprits, he argued, were the Bolshevik negotiators Mikhail Kalinin (1875–1945), chairman of the Kronstadt Soviet, and Nikolai Kuzmin, a commissar of the Baltic Fleet, who antagonized the rebels when a compromise was possible.

Serge was shocked at the lies the Bolshevik regime put out to defend itself, blaming the Kronstadt uprising on a fictitious White conspiracy. In the end he supported the government against the rebels, but without enthusiasm. He realized that the Kronstadt rebels could only succeed if they were supported by more conservative elements in Russian society. Their slogan of 'Soviet democracy' was utopian, he noted, but it 'lacked leadership, institutions and inspiration [and] at its back there were only masses of starving and desperate men'.[97] Nevertheless, the Kronstadt rebellion threw considerable light on the progress of the Revolution. A revolt by wealthy peasants – known as *kulaks*, meaning 'tight-fisted people' – could be disregarded, because the *kulaks* had never wanted socialism in Russia. But the Kronstadt sailors had been among the first to welcome the Bolshevik programme. Their disappointment and anger was a bitter blow.

For the next three years Lenin remained at the head of the government and the Bolsheviks attempted to appease their critics. For the next eight years a system of limited taxation was implemented so that the countryside could trade with the cities on the peasants' terms. Stock exchanges were opened and all attempts at state planning were reduced. Under the New Economic Policy (NEP) grain requisitions were abolished. All attention was focussed on the single question: what could the state do to appease the peasants and ensure that the cities were fed? If the period between 1917 and 1921 had been an attempt to turn Trotsky's theory of permanent revolution into reality, then the compromise years of 1921 to 1928 were closer to the spirit of the old Bolshevik formula of the democratic dictatorship of the proletariat and the peasantry.[98]

In an atmosphere of demoralization and defeat, several leading Bolsheviks were tempted to defend the status quo, as if they had secretly wanted it all along. The first theorist to speak of building 'socialism in one country' was Nikolai Bukharin, who argued that it was possible for a large independent economy to escape the influence of the world market. His ideal would have been an indefinite continuation of the New Economic Policy and his slogan for the peasants was 'Enrich yourselves!'[99] At least some good would have been done if the population was well fed. Bukharin's colleague, Joseph Stalin, made similar claims. They seemed a plausible enough justification for the very different Russia that his own policies would create.

This encouragement of a market economy was accompanied by a relaxation of censorship. Alternative viewpoints could be openly expressed, albeit indirectly, through art and literature. Trotsky even tried to make use of this slightly more liberal climate. In

Literature and Revolution (1924), for instance, he argues against those writers who believe that socialist literature should be written not only for the workers but by them. The first test of any work of culture, wrote Trotsky, was its success as art. Socialists could not legislate against cultural expressions that were complex or even hostile. Rather, they should thrust towards the society of the future, in which a new class of people, untainted by the memory of class exploitation, would create a new kind of art. Much later Trotsky's defence of artistic autonomy – as well as his fame as a revolutionary – brought him to the attention of a number of left-wing writers, artists and bohemians, including the French Surrealists around André Breton (1896–1966) and the Mexican Social Realist muralist Diego Rivera (1886–1957), *the man who painted walls.*[100]

In 1923 Trotsky began another project, liaising with educators, librarians, journalists and 'worker-correspondents'. Afterwards, he dedicated a book of essays, *Problems of Everyday Life: Creating the Foundations for a New Society in Revolutionary Russia* (1924), to the argument that Russia needed not only a political or economic revolution, but a spiritual one as well. If people stopped swearing, for instance, it would be a small sign that a revolution in outlook had been achieved. *A revolution does not deserve its name if it does not help with all its might and all the means at its disposal – if it does not help woman, twofold and threefold enslaved in the past, to get on the road of individual and spiritual progress. A revolution does not deserve its name if it does not take the greatest possible care of the children . . . for whose benefit it has been made. But how can one create . . . a new life based on mutual consideration, on self-respect, on the real equality of women . . . on the efficient care of children in an atmosphere poisoned with the roaring, rolling, ringing, and resounding swearing of masters and slaves?*[101]

The mid-1920s proved to be a period of limited but real reform. The secret police of the civil-war era, the Cheka, were abolished and replaced by a conventional force. The death penalty was again rescinded. But other areas of state supervision remained intact. The suppression of non-Bolshevik socialists continued and in 1921 the Communists introduced for the first time a ban on inner-party factions.[102] No attempt was made to restore the autonomy of the soviets, because the leading Bolsheviks were afraid that such platforms might prove hostile. Meanwhile the workers were too exhausted to recreate such institutions, whether pro- or anti- the regime. The New Economic Policy had begun as a temporary, limited measure, but its effects could be felt throughout Russian society. Everyone could see it was a compromise and further trouble was brewing.

One of the first signs of an impending crisis was the emergence of small opposition factions such as the Workers' Group of 1924. Headed by three old Communists with more than 75 years of party membership between them, the Workers' Group agitated for the restoration of Soviet democracy. Although the group was small in number, it had widespread support among rank-and-file Bolsheviks and there were calls for general strikes against the New Economic Policy. According to Deutscher, Trotsky 'did not see how the Government could meet the workers' demands: it was no use paying higher wages when wages could buy no

Joseph Stalin (1879–1953) was born Joseph Dzhugashvili in Georgia ('Stalin' means 'man of steel') and became a Marxist in the 1890s. In 1903 he joined the Bolsheviks under Lenin and was repeatedly imprisoned and exiled. In 1922 he became General Secretary of the Communist Party. After Lenin's death in 1924 he eliminated his rivals, including Trotsky, emerging as dictator in 1929. His Five-Year Plans to collectivize industry and agriculture were brutally enforced. Stalin's 1930s' reign of terror, culminating in the great purge, enabled him to increase his power. In the Second World War, after Hitler's invasion of the Soviet Union in 1941, Stalin reversed his 1939 alliance with Germany.

goods.' Trotsky took exception to the way in which the regime 'dwelt on the symptoms of the discontent instead of turning to the underlying cause', and when he saw Communists being instructed to denounce one another he was 'seized with disgust'.[103]

In March 1922 at the eleventh Party Congress the 52-year-old Lenin was visibly ill and tired. It was to be his last conference. At that same meeting Joseph Stalin was appointed General Secretary, an administrative post rather than a top leadership position. A one-time theology student, Stalin had played an undistinguished role in the Revolution and in the civil war, and there is no mention of him in *Ten Days That Shook the World*. 'Physically Stalin was unimpressive,' according to the historian William Taubman. 'Only about five feet six inches tall, he wore elevated shoes and stood atop a wooden platform on public occasions. His face was pockmarked; his teeth were uneven, his left arm and shoulder forever stiff from a childhood accident. His torso was too short and his arms too long. "It even makes him miserable", said Bukharin of Stalin, "that he cannot convince everyone, including himself, that he is a taller man than anybody else."'[104] Stalin was still widely regarded as a nonentity by most people in the party, including Trotsky who did not deign to regard him as a rival.

In May 1922 Lenin was paralysed by a stroke. In the final months of his life he wrote his political testament, aided by the

Lenin's political testament emphasizes the unsuitability for Russia of any system of individual rule. Trotsky was 'the most able man on the central committee,' he wrote, 'but he has too far-reaching self-confidence.' Bukharin 'is the Party's most valuable theoretician, but is too scholastic.' Zinoviev and Kamenev had proved their lack of nerve in 1917. No member of the leading party circles should be allowed to take too much power into their own hands, Lenin argued. Instead, leadership should be a collective task.

party's new General Secretary. As he worked more closely with Stalin, Lenin became increasingly wary of him. Stalin began to exert his authority. He purged the Communist Party in Georgia, accusing its leaders of giving too much support to local demands for regional autonomy. He also restricted the amount of access Lenin's wife, Nadezhda, could have to her husband. This period has been described as 'Lenin's last struggle'.[105]

The final codicil to the Soviet leader's Testament urged his comrades to remove Stalin at once from all positions of authority. It was too late. Lenin died in 1924 and, despite Nadezhda's protests, Stalin ensured that his final testament remained unpublished.

Trotsky was in the Caucasus recovering from an infection when he received a telegram. Lenin was fine, wrote Stalin, and Trotsky should stay just where he was.

Lenin's pallbearers 1923 identified by number are: 1 Kalinin 2 Bukharin 3 Zinoviev 4 Tomsky 5 Kamenev. Only Molotov (behind Zinoviev) would survive the years of Stalin (pictured far left)

The Revolution Betrayed (1923-1928)

Trotsky's survival at the head of the Soviet Union lasted only until Lenin's death. The next five years were marked by continuous conflict as various factions fought for supremacy.

On the right there was Bukharin, who argued for the continuation of the New Economic Policy. His allies looked for support from the wealthiest peasants and those who believed there could be some sort of compromise with the West.

On the left, Trotsky called for a resumption of the original international outlook of the regime. He and his allies wanted greater democracy in Russia and a reduction in the growing power of the state bureaucracy. Trotsky found greatest support among older Bolsheviks whose revolutionary activity predated 1917. Sections of the army backed him, as did many young workers and those who identified with his internationalist strategy, but they were already a small minority in the party.

Dominating the centre ground, for the time being, was Stalin, who claimed to believe in order, progress and stability. As General Secretary of the party he could veto appointments and his power base was the bureaucratic network. Those who supported Stalin did so because they worried that Trotsky was already too strong. Who was more likely to become Russia's Bonaparte than Trotsky, the founder of the Red Army? Even Kamenev, who was married to Trotsky's younger sister, Olga, backed Stalin, who also received the support of Zinoviev. Trotsky argued that Stalin's rule over bureaucracy meant nothing. Because the state played no role in production, its bureaucrats could not constitute a separate class. The real battle, he insisted, was between him and the right-wing Bukharin.

In 1923 Trotsky pushed forward his plans for democracy. *Pravda* published his articles advocating 'The New Course' in

Trotsky's sister Olga with her husband Lev Kamenev 1930

which he argued that a lack of internal debate prevented the party from meeting the needs of the time. *The essential, incomparable advantage of our party consists in its being able, at every moment, to look at industry with the eyes of the communist machinist, the communist specialist, the communist director and the communist merchant, collect the experience of these mutually complementary workers, draw conclusions from them and thus determine its line for directing the economy in general and each enterprise in particular. It is clear that such leadership is reliable only on the basis of a vibrant and active democracy inside the Party.*[106]

Trotsky's argument was linked to a specific moment in history, but his principles have a wider application. In any radical party, leadership can only succeed from vigorous democracy. There was one other criticism, however, which Trotsky held back from

The newspaper *Pravda* ('*Truth*') was originally founded as a workers' daily paper in 1912 in St Petersburg and became the official Communist Party newspaper in 1918.

making. If socialism requires democracy within the governing party, how can you have democracy inside the party unless views are also exchanged freely within society as a whole?[107] 'Destroying the multi-party system, the Bolsheviks had no inkling of the consequences to themselves,' notes Deutscher. 'They imagined that outside that system they would still remain what they had always been: a disciplined but free association of militant Marxists . . . The single-party system was a contradiction in terms: the single party could not remain a party in the accepted sense. Its inner life was bound to shrink and wither. No body politic can be nine-tenths mute and one-tenth vocal.'[108]

In May 1924 the Thirteenth Party Congress condemned Trotsky's faction and Zinoviev called for his removal from the party leadership. Stalin blocked that motion, for the time being. A year later Trotsky was removed from all military positions, the victim of a slander campaign that had Stalin's blessing. Various accusations were made. It was said that Trotsky had never been a proper Bolshevik, but was a mere journalist and dilettante, which is why he failed to appreciate the need for party unity. Even older memories were dredged up. Hadn't Trotsky slandered Lenin in the period after 1903? Wasn't he a Menshevik after all?

Playing to popular prejudice, doubt was cast upon Trotsky's racial origin. Wasn't there something rather cosmopolitan about his belief in global revolution? Would a true Russian have entertained such foreign ideas? To make matters worse, Trotsky appeared to go into hiding. Rather than speak at party meetings, he sat mute, reading French novels while others spoke. The party was degenerating and taking the Revolution with it, but Trotsky was powerless for as long as he lacked allies. There was nothing he could do but bide his time.

His speeches from this period cover many of the same themes as his *Problems of Everyday Life*, with the additional understanding that no revolution of people's mentalities could be achieved until

the spirit of 'bureaucratism' was overcome. *The rottenness of bureau-cratism consists of its disregard for the real tasks in hand and its evasion of what really needs doing, its sliding away at a tangent from what is essential – in the very times that compel us, as never before, to get to the essence, to the living heart of the matter, in every problem, big and small. A circular hard on the heels of another circular, itself followed by anoth-er circular, solves nothing – although we cannot do without circulars . . . We must not allow routine to settle down and harden; we must force open-ings in it that will let in better-worked-out methods; and allow new cre-ative possibilities to arise.*[109]

The greatest factor undermining Trotsky's authority was the obvious and increasing isolation of the Revolution. Internationalism had been the war-cry of the October Revolution. 'Complete and final victory,' wrote Lenin, 'cannot be achieved in Russia alone; it can be achieved only when the proletariat is victo-rious in at least all the advanced countries or, at all events, in some of the largest of the advanced countries. Only then shall we be able to say with absolute confidence that the cause of the proletariat has triumphed, that our first objective – the overthrow of capitalism has been achieved.'[110] The Communist International had been

The Commissar Vanishes – The image of Trotsky standing on the steps of the podium was removed from later prints of this photograph of Lenin addressing troops in Sverdlovsk Square 1920

formed to spread the Bolshevik's internationalist vision, but the world was not listening. In 1918 there had been a limited revolution in Germany, but the leaders of the Spartacus League were murdered the following spring and by the end of 1923 Germany had entered into a new period of conservatism and proto-Fascism.

The defeat of the German Communists was especially disheartening because Germany possessed the largest and most radical working-class movement in the world. For a moment, in 1923, a year of hyper-inflation, the idea of a revolution took hold again. Almost every organized group in German society seemed to go on strike simultaneously. A series of initiatives were debated to bring about a revolution, one of which was to invite Trotsky over on the sixth anniversary of the Russian Revolution to lead the German uprising. (Bukharin, Stalin and Zinoviev quickly moved to block that suggestion.) Despite such ideas, the German Communists were hampered by the memory of defeat. They lacked any clear plans for action or any idea of how to move the socialist-voting majority. And so the German revolution never happened.

Around this time one of Trotsky's oldest friends, Adolf Joffe (1883–1927), committed suicide. In a final letter to Trotsky, this long-standing and active member of the democratic opposition chided him for his lack of determination. Too often, wrote Joffe, Trotsky had held back from public criticism of Stalin's clique. Too often he had agreed to the wording of a compromise favourable to the party bureaucracy. 'Politically, you were always right, beginning with 1905,' he wrote, 'and I told you repeatedly that with my own ears I heard Lenin admit that even in 1905, you, and not he, were right. One does not lie before death and now I repeat this to you . . . You are right, but the guarantee of the victory of your rightness lies in nothing but the extreme unwillingness to yield, the strictest straightforwardness, the absolute rejection of all compromise; in this lay the very secret of Lenin's victories.' [111]

Joffe had spent some time in China as an envoy, advising Sun Yat-sen – the leader of the nationalist party, the Kuomintang – how to set up an army after he had overthrown the Qing dynasty in 1911. China had a nascent Communist Party at this time, but it was so small (it still had fewer than 1,000 members in 1925) that the Bolsheviks preferred to groom Sun, who was impressed with their forms of organization. In 1923 the Bolsheviks advised the Chinese Communist Party to join forces with the Kuomintang, but Sun's unexpected death in 1925 changed everything. Chiang Kai-shek became leader of the Kuomintang and he did not trust the Communists. Between 1925 and 1927 China was on the brink of revolution. A workers' movement emerged under Communist leadership and challenged the nationalists for power. Chiang Kai-shek responded by ordering nationalist troops to slaughter workers' uprisings in Canton and Shanghai. Thousands died and the workers' movement was brutally crushed.

From July 1926 onwards Trotsky threw himself into battle against Stalin. Working with Kamenev and Zinoviev in a United

Opposition, he addressed meetings and spoke before the Central Committee and the Politburo (the principal policy-making committee of the party). Victor Serge has left us with a moving account of this final struggle by the Opposition. 'I had no confidence that we would win,' he wrote. 'I was even sure in my own heart that we would be defeated. I remember saying this to Trotsky, in his big office at the Concessions Commission. In the old capital we could only count on a few hundred militants and the mass of the workers was indifferent to our case . . . As far as I was concerned everything was summed up in one conviction: even if there were only one chance in a hundred for the regeneration of the Revolution and its workers, democracy, that chance had to be taken at all costs.'[112]

In 1920 an emissary from the Comintern visited China to promote Communism. Only 12 people attended the inaugural Congress, one of them being the 28-year-old Mao Ze Dong (1893–1976). The Chinese Communist Party was founded in 1921 by two professors: Chen Duxiu (1879–1942) and Li Dazhao (1888–1927). In 1923 the party was encouraged by Moscow to join forces with the Kuomintang (the nationalist party), led by Sun Yat-sen (1866–1925). When Sun died suddenly in 1925 his successor Chiang Kai-shek (1887–1975) immediately moved to purge the Communists, whom he suspected of infiltrating the Kuomintang and urging peasants to revolt. In 1949 the Kuomintang was defeated by the Communists and a People's Republic was set up by Mao Ze Dong.

Some of the character of the Opposition at this time can be discerned from a leaflet written by Trotsky entitled 'The Russian Opposition: Questions and Answers' (1927). He identifies a series of problems facing the Soviet Union, from a bureaucratic attitude towards wages, unemployment and housing to the worsening condition of the poor, and goes on to hammer home his point that the main danger facing Russia is *bureaucratism*: the rise of a generation of bureaucrats whose obsession with power was strangling the Revolution from within. *The leaders of the ruling faction, who are iso-*

lating themselves to an ever-greater extent, prove incapable of estimating the situation as a whole, foreseeing the future and issuing broad directives to the Party. The policy becomes pettifogging or tail-endist. Attempts on anyone's part to generalize the difficulties, grasp their connection and look ahead into the future, arouse alarm in the conservative bureaucratic mind and call forth accusations of factionalism. The more difficulties in the economy and in politics the regime accumulates, the more intolerant it becomes.[113]

Trotsky accused the party leaders of cowardice and of being frightened of debate. *What the leaders of the ruling faction understand by the unity of the Party is the following: 'Don't you dare criticize our policy; don't dare pose any new tasks and new questions without our permission; don't dare to pose seriously the question of a struggle against bureaucratism, the question of industrialization, wages, poor peasants, etc.' From the standpoint of the leaders of the ruling faction, the unity of the Party is endangered by every word and every action that is directed against the mistakes of the leading group. But this only means that the leading group refuses to reconcile itself to a regime of party democracy.*[114]

Was Trotsky calling for an open system of popular democracy? Not yet. He was still using the language of Bolshevik continuity. *The Opposition stands for reinforcing the proletarian dictatorship, which is being weakened by shifts towards petty bourgeois elements. The dictatorship of the proletariat can be realized only through a party that is unified and capable of fighting. Various assertions to the effect that the Opposition is in favour of factions and groupings are lies spread for factional purposes.*[115] The logic of Trotsky's position was to argue for Soviet *reform*. The party could still be restored to a state of internal democracy, he said, and the link between the party and the workers re-established. All this could be achieved without the need for a new democratic movement to challenge the existing state. In response, Stalin did everything in his power to smear the Opposition, whereas Trotsky kept his gloves on.

What followed was in effect an ideological contest between two very different strategies for completing the Russian Revolution.

Trotsky was still convinced of the need for a truly international revolution. Stalin, on the other hand, argued that Russia could and should advance towards socialism on its own. His doctrine of 'socialism in one country' was a radical

> The real creation of a socialist economy in Russia will be possible only after the victory of the proletariat in the most important countries in Europe.
>
> LEON TROTSKY

departure from Leninism, merging Communism with Russia's national self-interest. After all, Lenin had said: 'We never harboured the illusion that the forces of the proletariat and the revolutionary people of one country – however heroic and however organized and disciplined they might be – could overthrow international imperialism. That can be done only by the joint effort of the workers of the world.'[116]

Stalin's 'socialism in one country' was also a rejection of Marx's belief that socialism was made possible, in part, by the resources accumulated under capitalism and would come about as a higher and more democratic society. But more important than Stalin's doctrinal heresy were the practical implications for the people of the Soviet Union. Stalin's success compelled them to live in conditions of isolation and blockade, under a leadership committed to the most extraordinary policies of shock industrialization. All resistance to Stalin would be met with implacable violence.

The Soviet bureaucracy was able to outmanoeuvre the Opposition, securing Trotsky's removal from the leading organs of the Russian Communist Party. Despite the fiasco of the German Spartacist revolt of 1919 and the even less promising uprising of 1923, the failure of the British General Strike of 1926 and of the so-called Chinese Revolution of 1927, Trotsky clung to his internationalist principles.[117] But as each revolt failed, Stalin and Bukharin gained in strength, while Trotsky's star waned. The final sign that Trotsky was now hopelessly isolated came during the tenth anniversary celebrations of the October Revolution. Trotsky and Zinoviev tried to appeal directly to the masses, but Stalin's henchmen blocked their way. Rather than protest at these strong-arm tactics, the crowd merely looked on passively.

The following year, 1928, Trotsky would be forced into exile. In time all of Stalin's rivals would be defeated: Zinoviev, Kamenev and even his former ally Bukharin.

From the winter of 1928–9 onwards, Stalin oversaw a new period of economic growth. The country's Five-Year Plan was amended to secure a vast increase of material goods (iron, steel, coal, oil and military supplies). In order to catch up with the more advanced economies of the West, Stalin made Russia take a crash course in industrialization. Huge factories were constructed and the peasants were ordered to abandon their individual farms so that they could be turned into collectives. Millions were forced into the cities, where living standards fell catastrophically. Stalin's plan had a grim simplicity: if people refused to work in slave conditions in the new industrial plants, let them starve – and millions did. Throughout the 1930s' the State's violence against the population increased day by day. As party leaders became ever more fearful of a popular rebellion or even of a low-level bureaucratic intrigue, millions more were rounded up and worked to death in Stalin's camps.

With the declared ambition of overtaking all advanced capitalist countries, Stalin set about copying the circumstances that had enabled their economies to boom. But while industrialization usually took place over centuries, Stalin allowed Russia just ten years. The whole country became one enormous factory and to enforce this economic experiment the state adopted such measures as forced labour, collectivization and imprisonment without trial. Socialism, the language of rebellion, had been abstracted, drained of all meaning and converted into a giant lie. 'Are we already living under 100 per cent Communism,' went a joke current at the time, 'or can things get worse?'

In January 1928 Stalin moved to secure Trotsky's deportation

In exile Trotsky and Natalia Sedova on a train from Esbjerg
to Copenhagen 1932

for counter-revolutionary activities. The date for his removal was
16 January. The Opposition continued to protest – and some
members even blocked the railway tracks to prevent Trotsky's
departure. The secret police arrived at his house, but the former
Bolshevik leader refused to let them in, forcing the officers to
break down his front door. By a strange coincidence, the man in
charge of the team had in fact served on Trotsky's military train
during the civil war. Confronted by his former leader, the soldier
broke down in tears and offered to take his own life. Eventually,
Trotsky was taken to the main railway station, where he engaged
in passive resistance. His son, Sedov, tried to stir the railwaymen
into action. 'Look comrades!' he cried. 'Look how they are carry-
ing off Trotsky!' Unmoved, the workers stared back in silence.[118]

Leon Trotsky was forced to live in exile for the remainder of his
life. From Turkey (1929–33), France (1933–5), Norway (1935–6)

and Mexico (1936–40) he wrote like a man possessed trying to explain to the world the various positions he and his supporters had taken. With his sons and some like-minded colleagues he edited the *Bulletin of the Opposition*, which was dedicated to the ongoing struggle of Soviet dissidents against the regime. In fact, much of the *Bulletin* was given over to obituaries of the many old Bolsheviks of 1917 who were picked off by Stalin one by one.

It was only after he had been forcibly expelled from Russia that Trotsky published his most famous book, *The History of the Russian Revolution* (1932). In it he takes pains to separate the noble ideals of 1917 from the tyranny of Stalin's rule. He starts with a history of the Russian monarchy and the conditions that shaped Tsarism, emphasizing the many ways in which pre-revolutionary Russia had fallen behind its rivals not only economically and militarily, but socially and culturally. This lack of development, he argues, also expressed itself in the characters of the Tsars. They were parochial, illiterate and ignorant of the Russian people over whom they ruled as dictators. But Russia's 'backwardness' was only half the story. Tsarist Russia had been a poor and under-developed country, but at the same time it had examples of the most modern techniques of production. This *combined and uneven development* revealed the dual character of Russian society.[119]

Trotsky's history of the Revolution proper begins with the revolts of February 1917 and ends with the October insurrection. He provides portraits of such leading characters as the former prime minister Kerensky and General Kornilov, but tends to minimize his own role in events, preferring to concentrate on the part played by Lenin.

He also defends the Revolution against those whom it deprived of power – such as Kerensky, who was now allied with the West. But he also wanted to show how Stalin's conduct had betrayed the democratic ideals of 1917. He did so by drawing attention to the quality of the movement at its height, rather than its subsequent decline. By challenging the existing order of Russian society, Trotsky argues, the October Revolution had created the potential for a totally different society in which the people directly participated. By promoting workplace soviets, the Bolsheviks had gone some way towards developing structures that enabled a system of direct popular rule, bringing these institutions closer to the people's will.

Trotsky's *History of the Russian Revolution* is one of the first great works of radical history. Most importantly, it portrays the Revolution as a process led by the Russian people. He always maintained that the successful advance of the Revolution never depended on the decisions of a few leaders, but came about through a succession of small but significant acts by anonymous individuals. From this perspective, the Tsar's abdication was a direct consequence of the first women bread-rioters to take to the streets in February 1917 and their bravery when faced by battalions of Cossacks. He devoted many pages to describing the rioters, who fraternized with the armed troops and thereby bridged the gap separating the state from the people. *The Revolution does not choose its paths*, wrote Trotsky, *it made its first steps towards victory under the belly of a Cossack horse.*[120]

He also made it clear that the willingness of the Bolsheviks to consider a second insurrection very much depended on the mood of the Petrograd workers, the sailors of Kronstadt and the soldiers in the garrison. The decision to overthrow the Provisional Government was the result of two main factors. The first was the absolute determination of key Bolshevik leaders to build a better society, including above all Lenin's *tension towards a goal*.[121] The second factor was the desire of Russia's cities for revolt. This willingness was manifested in Bolshevik majorities in the city soviets. The leader, Lenin, and the people worked together, guiding history towards its end. *The most indubitable feature of a revolution is the direct interference of the masses in historic events. In ordinary times the State . . . elevates itself above the nation and history is made by specialists in that line of business, kings, ministers, bureaucrats, parliamentarians, journalists. But at these crucial moments when the old order becomes no longer endurable to the masses, they break over the barriers excluding them from the political arena, sweep aside their traditional representatives and create by their own interference the initial groundwork for a new regime.*[122]

Trotsky's history of the Revolution distinguished itself from others because of its philosophical basis, its ambitious sweep and its open identification with the workers. Even the Tory historian A L Rowse was impressed, comparing Trotsky to his heroes Thomas Carlyle (1795–1881) and Winston Churchill (1849–95). 'The real importance of Trotsky's History,' he wrote, 'does not lie in his power of word painting, either of character or of scene, though indeed his gift is so brilliant and so incisive that one is continually reminded of Carlyle. There is something of the same technique, the same mannerism even, in the way the rapid lights shift across the scene and particular odd episodes are brought out in singular sharpness of relief and made to bear general significance; something of the same difficulty in following the sequence of events – the lights are so blinding – one may add. But where Carlyle had but his magnificent powers of intuition to rely on, Trotsky has a theory of history at his command, which enables him to grasp what is significant and to relate things together. The same point can be illustrated more appositely by comparison with Winston Churchill's *The World Crisis*, for the two men are not dissimilar in character and gifts of mind. But here again one notices the difference; for Mr Churchill's history, for all its personality, its vividness and vitality, points which it has in common with Trotsky – has not a philosophy of history behind it.'[123]

The American author Edmund Wilson (1895–1972) regarded Trotsky's book as a key moment in the writing of socialist history. For centuries, he argued, men had looked for patterns in the past. The first socialist historians took this approach further, arguing that historical development had a recognizable pattern. It followed that history was composed of grand impersonal forces that people could neither challenge nor shape. But Marx emphasized the ability of people to remake their world. 'Men make their own history,' he wrote in his *Eighteenth Brumaire* (1852), 'but they do not make it just as they please; they do not make it under circumstances chosen by themselves, but under circumstances directly encountered and inherited from the past.'[124] According to Wilson, the idea that people make history took over the socialist movement, so that the decisions of Lenin and Trotsky and the revolutionaries of 1917 could be explained as the choices of men who had 'identified history with themselves'.[125]

Indeed, a striking feature of Trotsky's character is the direct appeal he often made to the court of history. Remarks of this kind can be found in his speeches both at the height of his authority and in the years after. 'In contrast to Lenin,' wrote Lunacharsky, 'Trotsky is undoubtedly often prone to step back and watch himself. Trotsky treasures his historical role and would probably be ready to make any personal sacrifice, not excluding the greatest sacrifice of all – that of his life – in order to go down in human memory surrounded by the aureole of a genuine revolutionary leader.'[126]

At times Trotsky wrote as if in Marxism he had found a key to unlock all human development. His friends – and enemies – often chided him for his pride, which was linked to his sense of actively making history. On the other hand, the Russian Revolution would never have happened if a generation of radicals had not possessed the same overwhelming arrogance to say: 'I know how things are and I know how to change them for the better.'

A Tactic for Movement (1929-1933)

Trotsky is usually remembered as the man who led the October Revolution or as the founder of the Red Army. But he also defended the Revolution against its degeneration from within.

In exile, Trotsky was a major international figure as the one-time leader of a truly socialist state whose time might come again. His views on both Russian and international events were widely quoted and he played an important role in warning the world of the threat of Fascism. More clearly and urgently than anyone else, he explained the growing threat to the international left in Germany. Trotsky offered one remedy to the rise of Adolf Hitler – the anti-fascist unity of the workers of the world.

Trotsky had supported a socialist alliance for many years and from the early 1920s he had begun to use the term *united front*. At that time the Bolshevik state was secure, but the Revolution had failed to spread elsewhere. Although capitalist Europe had been convulsed by the fear of insurrection, its workers' movements were disorganized and inadequate. The Communist International had suggested that moderate socialists should split off from the main Communist parties because the moderates were still tainted by their role in the First World War. But by 1921 Europe's Communist parties had lost heart and the Bolsheviks encouraged them to work alongside the socialists, whenever such unity was in the interests of the workers. Unity was clearly lacking in the trade union movements, where the question of the workers' immediate needs was most sharply posed. An alliance of moderate socialists and Communists could only aid the class struggle.

How to persuade the masses to revolt? That was the question Trotsky asked in a 1922 speech. The answer varied according to the strength of the Communist parties in each country, yet throughout Europe Communists had opportunities to forge alliances with moderate socialists. *Most workers, he said, want the chance to struggle for a piece of bread, for a piece of meat. They see the Communist Party and the Socialist Party and do not understand why they have separated . . . Being in this state of mind and seeing in front of them various trade union and political organizations, they are disorientated. They are unable to prepare an immediate action, no matter how partial, how small. Then the Communist Party comes, and it says to them, 'My friends . . . we exist as independent parties for reasons that we, Communists, find completely legitimate. But despite everything, we Communists propose to you an immediate action for your piece of bread. We propose it to you, with you and your leaders, each organization which represents a part of the proletariat.' The tactic is completely in keeping with the mass psychology of the workers.*[127]

In several later works, Trotsky would draw on another early experience that seemed to demonstrate the usefulness of this tactic: the effective united front that was established between the Bolsheviks and Kerensky in the struggle against General Kornilov. Kerensky might have been *a lackey of the bourgeoisie*, but faced with a choice between the two men, the Bolsheviks had done the right thing. The main consideration had been to prevent Kornilov from *butchering the Petrograd proletariat*.[128] In the crucial months of autumn 1917 the Bolsheviks had not contented themselves with a general appeal to the workers and soldiers *to support the Red united front of the Bolsheviks. No, the Bolsheviks proposed the united front struggle to the Mensheviks and the Social Revolutionaries and created with them joint organizations of struggle.*[129]

There were, of course, several differences between these two situations. In 1922 the united front was proposed as a pact strictly between organized socialists and it was likely to involve some process of discussion and compromise. If left-wing and trade union politics dominated the terms of the alliance, then society would be pushed to the left. In 1917 the situation had been more desperate. Trotsky supported an alliance of the Bolsheviks not just with Social Revolutionaries on the left and the right and with Mensheviks, but even with Kerensky, a former socialist who had drifted far to the right and was now almost a dictator. The main difference between Kerensky and General Kornilov was that Kerensky still recognized the legality of some forms of revolution, while Kornilov wanted only to end the uprising as soon as possible.

Although there are essential differences between these two examples of a united front, there were also many similarities. In both cases the most important element was unity and that unity was broadly left wing. In each case, a united front was an expedient way of moving from a situation of difficulty or danger to a moment that would be more amenable to the left.

Trotsky's ideas could have proved most valuable in Germany. In the three years that preceded Hitler's rise to power Trotsky warned the European working class of the challenges they faced to halt the rise of Fascism. More immediately and with greater resolve than any of his contemporaries, he saw the extent of the dangers involved. Fascism's triumph could not be achieved without many more deaths. The victory of Hitler, he warned, would spell the end of the workers' movement in Germany, which possessed the strongest socialist left in Europe. *At the start of his political career, Hitler stood out only because of his big temperament, a voice much louder than others and an intellectual mediocrity much more self-assured . . . There were in Germany plenty of ruined and drowning people with scars and fresh bruises. They all wanted to thump their fists on the table. This Hitler could do better than others . . . Fascism has opened up the depths of society for politics . . . Everything that should have been eliminated from the national organism in the form of cultural excrement in the course of the normal development of society has now come gushing out from the throat; capitalist society is puking up the undigested barbarism. Such is the physiology of Nazism.*[130]

The first electoral successes of the National Socialist German Workers' Party (NSDAP) were achieved only in the period immediately following the Wall Street Crash of 1929. During the Great Depression unemployment soared and the votes of the main liberal parties collapsed. The Nazis portrayed 'Bolshevism' (meaning both Communists and socialists) as the single greatest obstacle standing in the way of the revival of the German nation. The leaders of the left-wing parties were

Adolf Hitler in a Nazi party shirt

aware of the threat and many of their followers grasped the need for a united front. What they lacked was any programme for united action. Such alliances as existed were small and localized and the majority of workers were not involved. In the absence of an anti-fascist unity, German politics witnessed a rapid succession of governing coalitions, each more reactionary than the last. The defeat of a Catholic-Socialist coalition in the winter of 1930 was followed by the removal of the elected Social Democratic government in the spring of 1932. By the end of that year parliament had virtually ceased to exist. A clique of former generals ruled Germany, the friends and colleagues of President Hindenburg (1847–1934).

The leaders of German Communism are much to blame for what happened next, although Stalinism aggravated the crisis. Following Hitler's first election victory in 1930 the leader of the German Communists, Ernst Thälmann, announced that this was

Ernst 'Teddy' Thälmann (1886-1944) led the German Communists from the late 1920s and was a consistent supporter of Stalin's line, even to his own cost. He stood against Hitler for the German presidency in 1932. He was arrested by the Nazis and murdered at the end of the war.

'Hitler's best day after which there would be no better, but only worse days.'[131] It was a hollow boast. Other leading Communists predicted that capitalism would be weakened by a brief period of Nazi rule. 'After Hitler, us!' went the slogan. Such notions had their origin in Stalin's domestic politics. He had defended his attack on Bukharin in 1929 by claiming the world was moving leftwards and capitalism was entering a 'third period' of revolutionary crisis. In Russia or Germany moderates belonged to the past. Under these circumstances, argued Stalin, social democracy was merely the last prop of capitalist tyranny. Reformist socialism was now the main obstacle to Communist success. Fascism and social democracy were not 'antipodes', in Stalin's notorious phrase, 'but twins'.[132]

The rank-and-file members of the socialist and Communist parties responded to the rise of Nazism with a mixture of fear and complacency. There was little hope of reconciliation for as long as the Communists continued to denounce socialists as 'social fascists'. In response, leading socialists were often more hostile towards the Communists than the Nazis.

Angered by the stupidity of the German Communists, Trotsky rushed into print, urging them to act. *Germany is now passing through one of those great historic hours upon which the fate of the German people, the fate of Europe, and in significant measure the fate of all humanity, will depend for decades*, began one article from late 1931. The Communists had to force the socialists into an alliance, he argued, and the united front had to involve millions of people. *The German worker has been raised in the spirit of organization and of discipline. This has its strong as well as its weak sides. The overwhelm-*

ing majority of the Social Democratic workers will fight against the fascists, but – for the present at least – only together with their organizations. This stage cannot be skipped. We must help the Social Democratic workers in action – in this new and extraordinary situation – to test the value of their organizations and leaders at this time, when it is a matter of life and death for the working class.[133]

Trotsky regarded Hitler as a menace to the world. *Fascism is a particular governmental system based on the uprooting of all elements of proletarian democracy within bourgeois society* and it planned *to smash all independent and voluntary organizations, to demolish all the defensive bulwarks of the proletariat and to uproot whatever has been achieved during three-quarters of a century by Social Democracy and the trade unions.*[134]

Trotsky's insistence upon social democracy connects this episode with his struggle for socialism in Russia. At one end of human experience was a situation of welfare and trade union democracy. At the other end was the world Hitler sought. But Trotsky's call for a united front was not purely defensive. The point was not just to protect the citadels of German socialism. He realized that a show of unity would bolster the confidence of the workers. If Fascism could be halted an opportunity might arise for a new offensive against Fascism and capitalism. In Trotsky's hands the idea of working-class unity in a defensive situation was a *strategic* good.

Copies of his pamphlets sold in hundreds of thousands. Breakaway parties were formed in Germany to the left of the socialists, but to the Right of the Communists, calling for 'united front' politics. Journalists and artists took up Trotsky's call. But in the end the party leaders were careful to prevent any rebellion among the rank and file. Hitler came to power on 30 January 1933 and within four months all leftist parties and trade unions had been banned. The decks had been cleared for the Second World War (1939–45) and the Holocaust.

Like Lenin in 1914 Trotsky at first refused to believe the news of this terrible defeat, but his attention was then distracted by a

Trotsky and his daughter Zina

domestic tragedy. The day after Hitler's victory, Trotsky received a letter from his first wife, Alexandra Sokolovskaya. She described to him the death of their daughter, Zina, and what she had said as she lay dying: 'It is sad that I can no longer return to Papa.'

'You know how I have adored and worshipped him from my earliest days. And now we are in utter discord. This has been at the bottom of my illness.' Alexandra chided her ex-husband for his inability to 'show your feelings, even when you would like to show them'. 'To those familiar only with the public face of Trotsky the passionate rhetorician,' observes Deutscher, 'his first wife's testimony about his undemonstrative intimate character may come as a surprise.'[135] If Trotsky was cold, it is possible that recurring misery had diminished some of his capacity to feel. Any spare emotional resources he might have had were poured into challenging the evils of Stalin, Hitler and war.

Over the next five years the crisis in Germany would be repeated elsewhere. In France and then in Spain a confident far right threatened to seize power. The left rallied in response, but its opposition was limited by the Communists, who still clung to slogans developed by the International. One difference was that the Comintern flipped over. Before 1933 its advice had always been broadly leftist: Communists should work with no one and make alliances with nobody, but simply wait. After 1935, however, the Comintern shifted far to the 'right'. Fascism was now seen as the most immediate and urgent threat and had to be fought. Yet rather than forge alliances primarily with socialist parties, the Communists in each country were now urged by the Comintern to make deals with anyone whatsoever – even groups on the fringes of Fascism. In Spain, for instance, they collaborated with the owners of factories, with army generals and the top brass of the police, conducting the revolution at the bosses' pace (which meant not at all). While the war against Fascism raged, the Communists set about jailing or killing the leaders of the authen-

The Spanish Civil War (1936–9) began as a military revolt by the Nationalist General Francisco Franco (1892–1975) against the Republican government of Manuel Azaña (1880–1940). By the end of 1936 the Nationalists controlled most of western and southern Spain and in 1937, aided by Italy and Germany, they captured Bilbao. In 1938–9 the Republicans lost Barcelona, Valencia and Madrid and Franco established a pro-Fascist dictatorship that lasted for more than 30 years.

tic Spanish left – independent socialists, anarchists and even a few Trotskyists were all purged. Once again, Trotsky leaped to the defence of the Revolution, warning that repression was no way to fight General Franco.

One of Trotsky's extraordinary talents was his ability to judge which elements of any situation were new. Following the 1905 Revolution, for instance, he grasped that the oppressive apparatus of Tsarism had been significantly weakened. While other exiles preferred to hold back and see which side would triumph, Trotsky threw himself into the fray. Although now living in exile, this talent remained with him, although in the spring of 1933 his prognosis was far less optimistic. Trotsky argued that the victory of Fascism would necessarily lead Europe into war. It was not that Fascism and capitalism were irreconcilable, but rather that Fascism demanded a change that could only come about through the warring of nations.

Earlier than anyone else Trotsky saw that Hitler's anti-Semitism was genuine and not merely a rhetorical device for stirring the masses. *It is possible to imagine without difficulty what awaits the Jews at the mere outbreak of the future world war*, he wrote in December 1938. *But even without war the next development of world reaction signifies with certainty the physical extermination of the Jews.*[136]

Following the forced resignation of the Austrian chancellor Kurt von Schuschnigg (1897–1977), Nazi forces entered Austria and Schuschnigg was imprisoned. The Germans declared Anschluss ('union') with Austria in March 1938.

Why could Trotsky see this when so many others could not? He had no special knowledge of the situation, but few people at the time believed the Nazis capable of genocide. Furthermore, the Jewish exodus from Germany only reached a mass scale after Hitler's annexation of Austria in 1938. Across the world the same mistakes were made and Hitler's enemies always underestimated him. While Trotsky was warning of the extermination of the Jews, Zionist representatives in Germany were still negotiating with the Nazi regime to ensure that German Jews would be sent from Nazi Germany to Palestine rather than Europe or America.

'I would not wish to be a Jew in Germany.'

GERMAN FIELD MARSHAL HERMANN GOERING (1893–1946), 12 NOVEMBER 1938.

Trotsky had no special interest in Jewish matters. He had grown up speaking Russian and some Ukrainian, but had never socialized with the Yiddish-speaking children of other local farmers. Neither his family nor his education led him to feel any strong ethnic ties. His prediction that the Jews would be exterminated was based simply on rational, political analysis. He saw that anti-Semitism was growing all over the world – in France, Russia and the United States. Austrian- or German-Jewish refugees were treated with little sympathy by other nations. If they were offered shelter, it was unwillingly. Usually they were barred from entering at all. At a time of serious economic crisis, capitalism was showing its most reactionary face. Meanwhile, the military successes of Hitler had radicalized the Nazi regime and all the signs pointed in one direction: war.

Zionism, the Jewish nationalist movement, emerged in the 1890s when the World Zionist Organization was founded. Its political aim was the establishment of a Jewish national home in Palestine and to this end it encouraged Jewish immigration. Some 60,000 German Jews arrived in Palestine from 1933 to 1939. The State of Israel was proclaimed in 1948.

The Last Struggle (1933–1936)

After leaving Turkey, Trotsky sought refuge in France in July 1933. The terms of his asylum were conditional: he could not take part in any political activity directed against the rulers of either France or Russia. The French Communist Party newspaper *l'Humanité* received notice of his arrival and called on all Communists to hunt down this traitor and saboteur. Nevertheless, Trotsky was able to find a modicum of peace. Rather than head for Paris, he and his entourage made for the village of Barbizon, near the forest of Fontainebleau. Unfortunately, after six months of quiet, the local police stumbled across Trotsky's messenger and the hostile press campaign resumed. From Germany Hitler's propaganda minister Joseph Goebbels (1897–1945) maintained that Trotsky was planning a new insurrection. The Communists described him as an enemy of the people and, once again, Trotsky was forced to move on.

Despite everything, he continued to write. Less well known than his *History of the Russian Revolution*, but equally important to him, was *The Revolution Betrayed* (1935), a sophisticated attempt to explain the Bolsheviks' defeat and Stalin's victory. According to Trotsky the cause of the Soviet state's degeneration was its very isolation: *The Soviet bureaucracy became more self-confident, the heavier the blows dealt to the world working class.*[137] In his view, Stalin's victory was made possible by the defeat of socialists in Germany, Britain, China and elsewhere. Stalin was a mediocrity who had not planned his rise to power; he had been handed it by others. *Before he felt out his own course*, wrote Trotsky, *the bureaucracy felt out Stalin himself*. The state officials were a new *ruling caste*.

The Russian Revolution had undergone a similar defeat to that suffered by the French Jacobins after 1793. Trotsky called this new period a *Soviet Thermidor*, from the name of the eleventh month in the French revolutionary calendar. Robespierre had been overthrown on the ninth of Thermidor (27 July) 1794 and the French government had shifted to the right, preparing the way for Napoleon Bonaparte (1769–1821) and the destruction of the First Republic. According to Trotsky, a similar thing had happened in Russia. Soviet democracy had been dismantled and the result was *a triumph of the bureaucracy over the masses*.[138] There was no equality in the Soviet Union when members of the privileged elite could secure living standards out of all proportion to the humble dwellings of the masses. Furthermore, on his way to the top Stalin had destroyed all democracy within the Russian Communist Party and the Communist International. Yet Trotsky maintained that the Soviet bureaucracy was not a ruling class. The class character of the Soviet Union had still to be *decided by history*.[139]

In Trotsky's view, the socialist system of State ownership was incompatible with bureaucratic rule. The bureaucracy would have to choose between returning to a private capitalist system or rediscovering its democratic roots. Unfortunately, Trotsky noted, *we cannot count upon the bureaucracy peacefully and voluntarily renouncing itself on behalf of socialist equality.* Were Stalin to rule unchallenged for a certain period of time, he predicted, the result would undoubtedly be the restoration of Western-style private capitalism. *Privileges have only half their worth if they cannot be transmitted to one's children. But the right of testament is inseparable from the right of property. It is not enough to be the director of a trust; it is necessary to be a stockholder.*[140]

The most likely outcome was that Stalin would establish permanent class privileges for the children of the new autocracy. But Trotsky predicted that the Russian people would surely resist such an obvious restoration of inequality. Some sort of movement for political reform would originate from within Soviet society, perhaps even from within the party itself. Certainly an upturn in the international workers' struggle would help; then, with or without the direct intervention of the Russian masses, the original goals of Soviet society might be restored.[141]

Trotsky was living in Norway when *The Revolution Betrayed* was published. The Norwegians had granted him asylum in the spring of 1935. At first he was even accorded a warm welcome by the leaders of the governing Labour Party, many of whom were former supporters of the Communist International. Yet once again trouble broke out. Norway's Communists and Fascists joined forces to demand that Trotsky be deported. It was then that he first heard about the Moscow show trials and the 'judicial' murder of an entire generation of old Bolsheviks. Leaned on by the Soviet Union, the Norwegian authorities kept Trotsky under house arrest. It was only when he was invited to live in Mexico by the radical government of General Lazaro Cardenas (1895–1970) that

A propagandist cartoon excoriates Trotskyist-Bukharin enemies of the people 1937

he saw a means of escape. He gratefully accepted and left Norway in December 1936.

In hiding or detention, Trotsky continued to write. Events in Moscow forced his name into the news and he was blamed for every setback in production, every timid official, every mistake that any Russian made. Meanwhile, other socialists were starting to speak out against Stalin. Several of Trotsky's contemporaries produced their own explanations of Stalin's rise, though most of them regarded it as an almost natural process, the inescapable consequence of mistakes made by the Bolsheviks long before. Karl Kautsky blamed everything on the dissolution of the Constituent Assembly. 'There exist only two possibilities,' he wrote, 'either democracy or civil war.' [142] In Friedrich Adler's view, the Bolsheviks had failed to place the workers' councils on a constitutional footing. [143]

In October 1916 the socialist Friedrich Adler (1879–1960) shot and killed Austrian Prime Minister Karl Graf von Stürgkh (1859–1916), who had governed without parliament during the war and was fiercely opposed by liberals and radicals. A physicist by profession, Adler won the support of Albert Einstein (1879–1955) for his actions. Released from jail during the revolutionary upsurge of 1918–19, Adler became a leader of the Austrian socialist party and then the Socialist International. The Austrians supported a rapprochement between socialists and Communists and even set up a mini 'International' of their own between the Second and Third Internationals. When they judged this to have failed, the Austrian socialists voted to return to the Second International.

Trotsky responded to these arguments in an essay entitled 'Stalinism and Bolshevism'. He listed the mistakes of which he was accused: the Bolsheviks should not have made concessions to the peasants or banned other political parties. All of these errors, he claimed, were the result of the Soviet Union's isolation. *The prohibition of other parties did not flow from any 'theory' of*

Bolshevism, he argued, *but was a measure of defence of the dictatorship on a backward and devastated country surrounded by enemies on all sides. For the Bolsheviks it was clear from the beginning that this measure – later completed by the prohibition of factions inside the governing party itself – signalled a tremendous danger. However, the root of the danger lay not in the doctrine or the tactics but in the material weakness of the dictatorship, in the difficulties of its internal and international situation. If the Revolution had triumphed, even if only in Germany, the need of prohibiting the other Soviet parties would have immediately fallen away. It is absolutely indisputable that the domination of a single party served as the juridical point of departure for the Stalinist totalitarian regime. The reason for this development lies neither in Bolshevism nor in the prohibition of other parties as a temporary war measure, but in the number of defeats of the proletariat in Europe and Asia.*[144]

This was the argument he had consistently used since 1905. The triumph or decay of revolutions was not arbitrary. It depended on brute historical fact. Socialism could not flourish in any one country and political isolation always resulted in tyranny, as had indeed happened. In other respects, however, the argument of 'Stalinism and Bolshevism' was an advance on the Opposition claims of ten years earlier. Trotsky was now willing to address the problem of democracy within the Soviet Union. He no longer made excuses for the system of Communist rule, but acknowledged that the democratization of the party must involve the opening up of society as a whole. There were other insights that only Trotsky of all his generation grasped. For Kautsky, Adler and others the most important explanation of Stalin's rise was that the Revolution had begun with violence, then terrorism had given rise to tyranny. The Russian workers played no part in either process. Only the laws of history could decide the result. Trotsky captured better than them a sense of the Revolution being *lost*.

As Trotsky continued to argue his case, news came to him of a vendetta that Stalin was waging against his family. His desperate daughter Zina had committed suicide in Berlin. Her husband Platon Volkov had disappeared. Trotsky's first wife, Alexandra, had been sent to a concentration camp where she died some time around 1938. His son, Sergei, a scientist with no political interests or connections, had been arrested on a trumped-up charge of poisoning the workers. He died in prison in 1937. The following year, Trotsky's other son Lev Sedov died in a hospital near Paris in a medical murder set up by Stalin's agents. Nobody was safe. When Trotsky was deported in 1929, his brother Alexander publicly disowned him, but he was still shot in 1938. Trotsky's sister Olga was married to Kamenev. Her two young sons were shot in 1936 and she suffered the same fate in 1941. Trotsky exposed these crimes in the *Bulletin of the Opposition* and they provide a very personal backdrop to his work.

Under the increasing pressure of events, Trotsky's tone became more radical than ever. Meanwhile Stalin made deals with every faction of the global ruling class and even, in 1939, the Nazis. It was around this time that Trotsky began work on his last full-length book: a biography of Stalin. Deutscher dismisses it as the least satisfactory of Trotsky's works and indeed some passages are inaccurate, others fantastical. Understandably, Trotsky lacked the sympathy towards his subject that he brought to his projected study of Lenin. But the undoubted strength of *Stalin* (1945) is its anger. *The current official comparisons of Stalin to Lenin are simply indecent*, he wrote. *If the basis of comparison is sweep of personality, it is impossible to place Stalin even alongside Mussolini or Hitler.*[145] In this biography Trotsky argues that Stalin butchered the Revolution, but even as he wrote, Stalin was at the height of his powers. Not for the first time, Trotsky appealed to future generations to come to his aid. After all, he added, the vicious Roman Emperor Nero (37–68 AD) had once been deified, but afterwards his statues were smashed to the ground and his name rubbed out. *The vengeance of history is more powerful than the vengeance of the most powerful General Secretary. I venture to think that this is consoling.*[146]

There were others in the Trotskyist movement who wanted to see

Joseph Stalin

this analysis pushed even further. All of his life Trotsky continued to insist that the condition of the Russian state had still not been decided by history and many of the terms he used to characterize Stalinist society were deliberately provisional. He argued that the rulers of Soviet Russia remained a group, rather than a caste or a class. But this leaves several unanswered questions. How many years would it take before they deserved to be called a class or caste? Trotsky insisted that the workers' state had been 'deformed', but by how much? And at what stage should socialists regard the Soviet Union as a hostile entity?

There were many on the Left who maintained that the Russian Revolution had become another tyranny, a bureaucratic form of state capitalism.[147] Trotsky's decision to launch a Fourth International was a practical way of recognizing the negative part played by the Communist parties internationally. But he still maintained that the state ownership of property in the

Soviet Union kept it a society apart. After Trotsky's death – and while the Soviet Union continued to flourish – he was often criticized for taking this position. Yet even now we should appreciate the spirit in which such complaints were made. Those who took seriously the practical imperative of Marxism to change the world learned much from Trotsky, even if they sometimes criticized him in print.

In his last years Trotsky began to keep philosophical notebooks, many of them taken up with an analysis of the different temperaments of Martov and Lenin. For all Martov's learning and sophistication, he argued, Lenin was undoubtedly the greater man. *The inflexible, 'doctrinaire', 'scholastic' Lenin indefatigably learned from events,* he wrote, *but the realist Martov created for himself a lofty refuge from the action.* [148] Trotsky had undoubtedly modelled himself on both men at different times in his youth; Martov perhaps even more than Lenin. Later he hoped to publish a biography of Lenin that would demonstrate once and for all the difference between Lenin's theories and Stalinist autocracy. This project remained largely incomplete in his lifetime, although the drafts of a manuscript were published. [149]

In another book, *Their Morals and Ours* (1938), Trotsky rejects the criticism often levelled at him that the Bolsheviks always privileged ends over means. Opponents of the Revolution liked to point out that the regime had resorted to terror, believing that the end – socialism – justified the means. Trotsky's response was that Marxists had never thought in this way. They believed that the ends *were* the means.[150] He had opposed Stalin because he realized that the use of terror would lead to dictatorship.

The publication of *Their Morals and Ours* brought Trotsky into conflict with his French translator, Victor Serge. It was a bitter farce. Serge had survived imprisonment under Stalin, escaped to Europe and allied himself with Trotsky in exile. The best known and most gifted of Trotsky's remaining allies, Serge was accused of adding a hostile prospectus to the book that mutilated Trotsky's argument. It was a ludicrous charge and also a sign that Comintern agents had infiltrated Trotsky's inner circle, an inward-looking, often paranoid clique.[151]

Despite his personal hardships Trotsky continued to criticize the degeneration of the Revolution, Stalin and the leaders of the Soviet Union and the bullying tactics adopted by the Communist International. His intervention was most necessary in France and Spain. Between 1930 and 1933 the Stalinists had made great efforts to persuade ordinary Communists that the socialists were their greatest enemy. After 1935, however, the various Communist parties lurched to the right. Now they were encouraged to set up permanent alliances – a popular front – not just with socialists, but with liberals and even some right-wingers on the fringes of Fascism. Trotsky denounced the popular front in favour, as ever, of a working-class united front.[152]

As far as Trotsky was concerned, his most important task was the organization of those like-minded militants who also rejected Stalinism. Some figures who would later play an important part in this movement were long-standing friends. Early members of the Russian Opposition included Karl Radek and Christian Rakovsky, while Alfred Rosmer played a similar part in France. Others knew Trotsky from the early 1920s, including the American journalist Max Eastman. Radicals in many countries opposed the bureaucratic campaign against Trotsky's Opposition. The alliance with Grigori Zinoviev and Lev Kamenev brought the early 'Trotskyists' into alliance with other dissidents such as Arkadi Maslow (1891–1941) and Ruth Fischer (1895–1961) in Germany. Sporadic alliances were made with other groups of oppositionists, like those in sympathy with Bukharin (including August Thalheimer (1884–1948) in Germany) or the Italian leftist Amadeo Bordiga (1889–1970).

Before 1933, however, any co-operation was purely *ad hoc*.

Trotsky always insisted that the only hope for revolutionary change lay with the forces of the Communist International. When friends or allies were expelled from Communist parties – as happened to Rosmer and Pierre Monatte in 1924 – they were urged by Trotsky to make their peace, close down their independent publications, return to these parties and change them from within.[153]

However, the destruction of the German working class by Fascism changed Trotsky's tactical thinking. He recognized 1933 – the year in which Hitler became chancellor – as a great defeat, a date in world history as important for posterity as 1917. It was following the betrayal of the German working class that Trotsky called for a Fourth International untainted by the mistakes of the Communist International that had preceded it. He also made attempts to work with other non-Stalinist organizations.

New socialist parties were established in most countries, but few of them had mass appeal. Manifestos were written and a programme of 'transitional' demands was adopted so as to resolve a contradiction in the habits of previous socialist parties. In the old parties a 'revolutionary' programme co-existed unevenly alongside the search for 'reformist' demands and, in practice, the Revolution was sidelined in favour of small reforms. The idea of a transitional programme was to make modest-sounding demands (a minimum wage, for example) that were unacceptable to capitalism at the time. This would illustrate the distinctive character of their movement and point the way towards revolutionary change. Unfortunately, Trotsky's supporters lacked the numbers or the influence to realize such a programme.

Many revolutionaries were hostile to Trotsky's call for a Fourth International. The rise of Fascism encouraged local activists to lie low in existing groups and Trotsky was the subject of outrageous personal slanders. In truth, few people wanted to go through the process of beginning all over again so soon after the formation of the Communist International. Trotsky maintained he was right,

Born in the Caribbean, Cyril Lionel Robert James (1901–89) left Trinidad in 1932, becoming a prominent journalist, writer and political activist in Britain. He is best known for his history of *The Black Jacobins* (1938), a study of the revolutionary Haitian movement that defeated the slave trade. He met Trotsky in exile and spent several years as a member of various American Trotskyist groups. James later broke with them, arguing for a Marxism influenced by the categories of Hegel and Lenin. His writing influenced a generation of African leaders such as Jomo Kenyatta (1889–1978) and Kwame Nkrumah (1909–72).

however, guided in part by the memory of Zimmerwald. Those tiny gatherings of 1915 had resulted in a large Communist movement by the early 1920s and he was convinced his Fourth International could grow just as rapidly. But he failed to see that world events were conspiring against him. Few of his followers shared his belief that destiny would come to their rescue.

The Trotskyites made the best of a bad job. By the time of his death, Trotsky's American supporters had recruited around a thousand members, including prominent intellectuals and working-class militants whose experience went back to the founding days of the US Communist Party in 1919. Even larger parties were later established in Belgium, Ceylon (modern Sri Lanka) and elsewhere. Nevertheless, progress was painfully slow.

Activists of the stature of Victor Serge and later C L R James found this whole cycle dispiriting. Many of the Trotskyist parties were small, consisting of only a handful of activists. Those who were initially attracted to such parties were often bohemians, writers, artists or intellectuals who valued Trotsky's individual stance, but were not rooted in the workers' movement, which placed them at a marked disadvantage compared to their Stalinist opponents. Like all small parties the Trotskyists were also prone to factionalism. The left-wing British historian and activist Duncan Hallas (1925–2002) blamed Trotsky: 'Trotsky encouraged the various sections of the opposition to interest themselves in each others' activities; he wrote interminable circulars and epistles explaining, say, to the Belgians why the French fell out, to the Greeks why the German comrades were in disagreement, to the Poles what were the points at issue between different sets of the Belgian or of the American opposition, and so on and so forth . . . Some of this was doubtless unavoidable, a necessary consequence of the propagandist stance which, in turn, was politically correct at the time. Some but by no means all. Trotsky's method legitimized and encouraged the pretensions of people who, though they could not gain so much as a toehold in their own working-class movement, felt able to pronounce on the details of tactics and policy all over the world. It fostered the very "conceit and grand airs" that was such an obstacle to serious work.'[154]

The Fourth International styled itself 'The World Party of the Socialist Revolution', although Trotsky was very aware of the problems it faced. Every attempt to change the world only seemed to make it worse. Frustrated by current events, he tended to praise the historical role of his comrades in an exaggerated fashion. Crisis was all about and only a determined leadership could save the day: *The epoch . . . about to begin for European humanity will not leave a trace in the labour movement of all that is ambiguous and gangrened . . . The sections of the Second and Third International will depart the scene without a sound, one after the other. A new and grand regrouping of the workers' ranks is inevitable. The young revolutionary cadres will acquire flesh and blood.*[155]

In retrospect, the horrors of the Second World War have given some of Trotsky's exaggerated warnings a veneer of justification. On the other hand, we should not fall into the trap of assuming that Trotskyism was a mere fantasy or an irrelevance. It provided some sort of continuity with the radicalism of the early twentieth century and it created a space within which a genuinely original Marxism could begin to develop. Without Trotskyism the left would have had to start from scratch in 1945. We can also compare those countries where Trotskyism had some presence, no matter how uncertain, before 1968 (such as France and Britain) with those where it was missing and other leftist traditions, including Maoism and terrorism, filled the gap (such as Germany and Italy).

In the late 1930s one of the most important tasks was to defend Trotsky during Stalin's show trials. In three major cases between 1936 and 1938 the best of the old Bolsheviks were tried: Kamenev, Zinoviev, Bukharin and Radek were all found guilty. Trotsky was the missing defendant. He was accused *in absentia* of espionage, sabotage and generally masterminding a conspiracy in an omnipotent manner! Like a trained parrot Zinoviev told the court: 'My defective Bolshevism became transformed into anti-Bolshevism and through Trotskyism I arrived at Fascism. Trotskyism is a variety of Fascism and Zinovievism is a variety of Trotskyism.'[156] Almost none of Lenin's former colleagues had the courage to deny the charges. Instead they showed a mistaken loyalty to the Party of 1917. Most of the old Bolsheviks had already recanted and they were too far along this road to stop now. Others were motivated by loyalty to the party. Although their own lives would be lost, they could see no alternative to Communism. Had they won, it would have meant the defeat of the Party, which was unthinkable.

Indeed it is striking how few of the old Bolsheviks ever challenged the system. Bukharin was used in the 1980s as a symbol of 'socialism with a human face'. But far from opposing Stalin in the 1920s, Bukharin's elaboration of the theory of 'socialism in one country' actually handed the General Secretary the ammunition he needed to defeat Trotsky. Kamenev and Zinoviev vacillated, capitulating to Stalin at the start and end of the 1920s and submitting meekly to the show trials. At least Bukharin fought back in court, though he was still executed.[157]

We might also look at the example of Alexandra Kollontai.

A rare survivor Alexandra Kollontai conducted the peace negotiations that ended Soviet-Finnish hostilities during the Second World War. Photographed here in Sweden where she was Soviet Ambassador 1945

The leading Bolshevik expert on women's politics, she became one of the first Russian dissidents, supporting opposition platforms from the early 1920s. Naturally she came under sharp attack from the party majority, but she held firm to her beliefs.[158] Yet faced with the rise of Stalin she hid away in the state bureaucracy. She was posted as ambassador to Norway in 1922 and from there to Mexico (1926–7), then Norway again (1927–30) and finally Sweden (1930–45). No one familiar with her work could dismiss her long struggle for women's rights and workers' democracy (which she regarded as inextricably linked), yet if we do champion her as an early advocate of Soviet democracy, we must also acknowledge Trotsky as the greater rebel.

It was not only exile that defended Trotsky from a similar fate, but the nature of his politics. He continued to fight, no matter how wretched the situation. In response to the show trials he published letters and pamphlets proving that Stalin's accusations were inconsistent, impossible and absurd. His supporters established a commission to judge the truth or otherwise of the charges, with the liberal philosopher John Dewey (1859–1952) in the chair. Dewey, who had no time for Trotsky's politics, took the charges seriously, but after much debate he found Trotsky innocent of every one.

Dewey's verdict received only muted publicity. Most activists on the left had retreated into the shells of existing organizations and Trotsky was *persona non grata*. This is how he was described at the fifteenth congress of the British Communist Party in 1935: 'Every weak, corrupt or ambitious traitor to socialism within the Soviet Union has been hired to do the foul work of capitalism and Fascism . . . In the forefront of all the wrecking, sabotage and assassination is the fascist agent Trotsky. But the defences of the Soviet people are strong. Under the leadership of the Bolshevik Comrade Yezhov, the spies and wreckers have been exposed before the world and brought to judgement.'[159] Incidentally, the unfortunate Yezhov was 'purged' a mere twelve months later.

The majority of Communists in Europe were convinced that the Moscow show trials were fair. They preferred not to face up to the

unpleasant truth that the trials were rigged and they were being lied to and manipulated by the Soviet regime. For this reason, despite all of their energetic work, the Trotskyists possessed no more members in 1938 than they had four years before.

Wilhelm Schulz cartoon of Trotsky after his fall from favour. 1928

Mexico (1937–1940)

'Whence did he draw his energy, his physical endurance?' Trotsky's second wife, Natalia, later wondered. 'Neither the unbearably hot sun, the mountains nor descents with cacti heavy as iron bothered him. He was hypnotized by the consummation of the task at hand. He found relaxation in changing his tasks. This also provided him with a respite from the blows which mercilessly fell upon him. The more crushing the blow the more ardently he forgot himself in work.'[160]

The last flight. Trotsky and Natalia arrive in Mexico January 1937

Trotsky's friends and patrons
Diego Rivera and Frida Kahlo,
New York 1933

Other friends and colleagues remember Trotsky in Mexico. Joseph Hansen (1910–79), a young member of the American Opposition, drove a new Dodge sedan from Ohio to Mexico in 1937 to join Trotsky's small staff of secretaries and guards. He was nervous about meeting the legend in the flesh. 'In my eyes Trotsky was one of the giants of history, looming so large that he seemed like a remote figure, belonging to another age.'[161] Hansen had been warned that the 58-year-old Trotsky could be a remote and difficult employer, so he was pleasantly surprised when he warmly embraced him on his arrival. 'He wanted to know about our trip and how the comrades were in New York.'[162]

Hansen has left a fascinating account of Trotsky through the eyes of a loyal subordinate. He tells us that Trotsky only wrote articles for the press with the utmost reluctance and that the Mexican muralist Diego Rivera and his wife the painter Frida Kahlo (1907–54) were frequent visitors. 'LD [Lev Davidovich or 'Trotsky'] was strongly attracted to Diego,' he wrote, 'to the imagination, charm, transparency and geniality of the great artist.'[163] (Trotsky's physical attraction to Frida might also have played a part.) Rivera had helped convince the Government to invite Trotsky to live in Mexico, but sadly their friendship was broken when Rivera supported a parliamentary candidate

Trotsky's grandson Esteban Volkov stands at his graveside in Mexico

who campaigned falsely as Trotsky's representative.

In his time as Trotsky's assistant, Hansen also joined the campaign against the Moscow show trials. 'Working with Trotsky was a serious matter,' he noted. 'He was no dabbler in politics and he found dabbling intolerable in others; but it was also an extraordinary school for the young comrades on his staff.'[164]

In Mexico Trotsky was able to say what he liked and go where he liked, though this new freedom had its dangers. Stalin wanted him dead and had given

The attack came at 4 a.m. I was fast asleep, having taken a sleeping drug after a hard day's work. Awakened by the rattle of gunfire but feeling hazy, I first imagined that a national holiday was being celebrated with fireworks outside our walls. But the explosions were too close, right here within the room, next to me and overhead . . . The shooting continued incessantly. My wife later told me that she helped me to the floor, pushing me into the space between the bed and the wall . . . Splinters of glass from windowpanes and chips from walls flew in all directions. A little later I discovered that my right leg had been slightly wounded in two places. As the shooting died down we heard our grandson in the neighbouring room cry out 'Grandfather!' The voice of the child in the darkness under the gunfire remains the most tragic recollection of that night.

TROTSKY, 'STALIN SEEKS MY DEATH', JUNE 1940[165]

orders to the People's Commissariat of Internal Affairs (NKVD) for Trotsky to be assassinated. In May 1940 a first attempt was made to kill him: his house at Coyoacan was sprayed with gunfire. Trotsky escaped with his life, but it was only a matter of time before somebody succeeded.

In September 1939 the Spanish Communist Jaime Ramon Mercader (1914–78) arrived in New York, though his passport (taken from a dead Canadian volunteer in the International Brigade) bore the name 'Frank Jacson'. Travelling to Mexico City, Mercader made contact with local Soviet agents and on 24 May he made Trotsky's acquaintance for the first time. 'Frank Jacson' visited Trotsky's well-guarded home a total of ten times, bringing chocolates and gifts and offering to take the family climbing in the hills. In conversation he adopted a friendly but sceptical manner that appealed to Trotsky's love of the chase. 'Jacson' would never be a good comrade, Trotsky told his friends, but perhaps he would give money or some other support to the cause.

As the final act approached Mercader was often ill. He spent many days in bed and Trotsky's guards noticed that the visitor had begun to sweat profusely. Trotsky, in contrast, appeared in the best of health. Waking up on the morning of 20 August 1940 he told Natalia: 'You know, I feel fine today, at all events, this morning; it's a long time since I felt so well.' [166] At 1 p.m. he was visited by his attorney. After a brief siesta, Natalia saw Trotsky sitting at his desk in his study. 'He continued to be in good spirits,' she recalled. 'And it made me feel more cheerful . . . Every now and then I opened the door to his room just a trifle, so as not to disturb him, and saw him in his usual position, bent over his desk, pen in hand.'[167]

At 5.20 p.m. 'Jacson' called. Natalia answered the door and later recounted their conversation:

'"I'm frightfully thirsty, may I have a glass of water?" he asked, upon greeting me.

'"Perhaps you would like a cup of tea?"

'"No, no. I dined too late and feel that the food is up here," he answered, pointing at his throat. "It's choking me." The colour of his face was grey-green. His general appearance was that of a very nervous man.

'"Why are you wearing your hat and topcoat?" (His topcoat was hanging over his left arm, pressed against his body.) "It's so sunny today."

'"Yes, but you know it won't last long, it might rain."

'I wanted to argue that "today it won't rain" and of his always boasting that he never wore a hat or coat, even in the worst weather, but somehow I became depressed and let the subject drop.'[168]

'Jacson' had brought with him an article for Trotsky to read. He walked upstairs to the study where his victim was still sitting at his desk. As they were talking, Mercader walked behind Trotsky, took an ice pick from a coat pocket and buried it in the old man's head.

'Trotsky gave a cry that I shall never forget,' Mercader later recalled. 'It was a long "aaaa", endlessly long, and I think it still echoes in my brain. Trotsky jumped up jerkily, rushed at me and bit my hand. Look, you can still see the marks of his teeth. I pushed him away and he fell to the floor. Then he rose and stumbled out of the room.'[169]

Hearing her husband's cries, Natalia ran to him: 'Between the dining room and the balcony, on the threshold, beside the door post and leaning against it stood . . . Lev Davidovich [Trotsky]. His face was covered with blood, his eyes, without glasses, were sharp blue, his hands were hanging.

'"What happened? What happened?"

'I flung my arms about him, but he did not immediately answer. It flashed through my mind. Perhaps something had fallen from the ceiling — some repair work was being done there — but why was he here? And he said to me calmly, without any

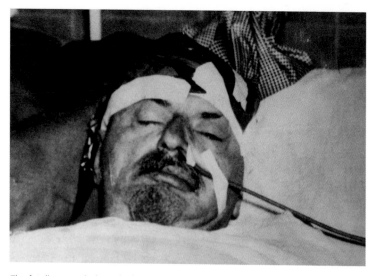

The fatally wounded Trotsky lies dying in a Mexico City hospital

indignation, bitterness or irritation, "Jacson". LD [Trotsky] said
it as if he wished to say, "It has happened."'[170]

Trotsky fell into a coma and died the following day, 21
August 1940. He was buried in Mexico and large crowds gath-
ered to watch the funeral procession in Mexico City.

Ramon Mercader was arrested and sentenced to 19 years in prison.
He was released in 1960 and decorated by the Soviet Union.[171]

Shortly before he died, Trotsky had written his own political
Testament. He and Natalia were alone in a strange country. A
world war was being waged in which tens of millions of people
would certainly perish. He had campaigned to end the First World
War, but was powerless to prevent this new one. His health was
failing and he expected death to come soon, one way or another. He
could not have known the precise manner of his end, but many of
his friends and family had been murdered by the Soviet regime and
he knew that Stalin regarded him as enemy number one.

Despite all this, Trotsky's Testament is not a gloomy document and it ends with a heartfelt expression of hope in the future.

My high (and still rising) blood pressure is deceiving those near me about my actual condition, he wrote. *I am active and able to work, but the outcome is evidently near. These lines will be made public after my death.*

I have no need to refute here once again the stupid and vile slander of Stalin and his agents: there is not a single spot on my revolutionary honour. I have never entered, either directly or indirectly, into any behind-the-scenes agreements or even negotiations with the enemies of the working class. Thousands of Stalin's opponents have fallen victims of similar false accusations. The new revolutionary generations will rehabilitate their political honour and deal with the Kremlin executioners according to their deserts.

I thank warmly the friends who remained loyal to me through the most difficult hours of my life. I do not name anyone in particular because I cannot name them all.

However, I consider myself justified in making an exception in the case of my companion, Natalia Ivanovna Sedova. In addition to the happiness of being a fighter for the cause of socialism, fate gave me the happiness of being her husband. During the almost forty years of our life together she remained an inexhaustible source of love, magnanimity, and tenderness. She underwent great sufferings, especially in the last period of our lives. But I find some comfort in the fact that she also knew days of happiness.

For forty-three years of my conscious life I have remained a revolutionist; for forty-two of them I have fought under the banner of Marxism. If I had to begin all over again I would of course try to avoid this or that mistake, but the main course of my life would remain unchanged. I shall die a proletarian revolutionist, a Marxist, a dialectical materialist, and, consequently, an irreconcilable atheist. My faith in the Communist future of mankind is not less ardent, indeed it is firmer today, than it was in the days of my youth.

Natalia has just come up to the window from the courtyard and opened it wider so that the air may enter more freely into my room. I can see the bright green strip of grass beneath the wall and the clear blue sky above the wall, and sunlight everywhere. Life is beautiful. Let the future generations cleanse it of all evil, oppression and violence, and enjoy it to the full.[172]

Notes

1   D Volkogonov, *Trotsky: The Eternal Revolutionary* (London: Harper Collins, 1994); I Deutscher, *The Prophet Unarmed: Trotsky 1921–1929* (Oxford University Press, 1959), p.509.
2   A Lunacharsky, *Revolutionary Silhouettes* (London: Penguin, 1967), p.65.
3   L Trotsky, *My Life: An Attempt at an Autobiography* (London: Penguin, 1975), p.1.
4   L Trotsky, *The Young Lenin* (London: Penguin, 1972), pp.104–20.
5   Trotsky, *My Life*, p.3.
6   M Eastman, *Leon Trotsky: The Portrait of a Youth* (London: Faber and Faber, 1926), Chapter 3.
7   Ibid.
8   Trotsky, *My Life*, p.19.
9   I Deutscher, *The Prophet Armed: Trotsky 1879-1921* (London: Oxford University Press, 1954) p.12.
10 Trotsky, *My Life*, p.45.
11 Ibid., p.50
12 Trotsky's critique of Narodnik terrorism appears in L Trotsky, *Marxism and Terrorism* (New York: Pathfinder Press, 1995), pp.7–12.
13 L Trotsky, 'A Note on Plekhanov', *Fourth International*, 7–11 March 1943, pp.92–4.
14 'An Estimate of Marx by International Liberalism', in V I Lenin, *Collected Works: Volume 13* (London: Lawrence and Wishart, 1960), pp.490–5.
15 Cited in Deutscher, *The Prophet Armed*, p.25.
16 Trotsky, *My Life*, pp.110–2.
17 Deutscher, *The Prophet Armed*, p.28.
18 Ibid.
19 Trotsky, *My Life*, pp.110–2.
20 Deutscher, *The Prophet Armed*, p.30.
21 Trotsky, *My Life*, p.112.
22 Deutscher, *The Prophet Armed*, p.31.
23 Peter Struve, RSDLP Manifesto.

24 'What Is to Be Done? Burning Questions of Our Movement', in V I Lenin, *Collected Works: Volume 5* (London: Lawrence and Wishart, 1961), pp.347–530, 464.

25 M Liebman, *Leninism Under Lenin* (London: Merlin Press, 1975).

26 Ironically, Trotsky's earliest views on organization were prematurely 'Leninist'. See Deutscher, *The Prophet Armed*, p.45.

27 Trotsky, *My Life*, pp.140–1; Deutscher, *The Prophet Armed*, p.55.

28 Trotsky, *My Life*, p.137.

29 Deutscher, *The Prophet Armed*, p.55.

30 V Serge, 'La vie Intellectuelle en Russie: Un portrait de Lénine par Trotsky', *Clarté* 75 (1925), pp.255–8.

31 Trotsky, *My Life*, pp.152.

32 Robert Harvey, *Comrades: The Rise and Fall of World Communism* (London: John Murray, 2003), pp.43–4.

33 See 'Trotsky on Substitutionism', in T Cliff, *Neither Washington nor Moscow: Essays on Revolutionary Socialism* (London: Bookmarks, 1982), pp.192–209, 199.

34 Serge, 'Un portrait de Lénine par Trotsky', pp.255–8.

35 Trotsky, *My Life*, pp.166–7.

36 P Pomper (ed), *Trotsky's Notebooks 1933–1935: Writings on Lenin, Dialectics and Evolutionism* (New York: Columbia University Press, 1986), pp.94–5.

37 Deutscher, *The Prophet Armed*, pp.111–12.

38 T Cliff, *Trotsky 1879–1917: Towards October* (London: Bookmarks, 1989), pp.80–7; Deutscher, *The Prophet Armed*, p.104.

39 Lunacharsky, *Revolutionary Silhouettes*, p.65.

40 Trotsky, *My Life*, p.188.

41 I Howe, *Trotsky* (London: Fontana, 1978), p.26.

42 Trotsky, *My Life*, pp.196–7.

43 K Marx and F Engels, 'Address of the Central Authority to the League, March 1850', in *Marx and Engels Collected Works: Volume 10* (London: Lawrence and Wishart, 1978), pp.277–87, 281.

44 Two of Trotsky's speeches on the idea of European socialism have been published as L Trotsky, *Europe and America: Two Speeches on Imperialism* (New York: Pathfinder Press, 1971).

45 L Trotsky, *The Permanent Revolution* (New York: Pathfinder Press, 1969). The extract here is taken from L Trotsky, 'Permanent Revolution', http://www.marxists.org/archive/trotsky/works/1931-tpv/index.htm.

46 From 'Europe and Revolution', in Trotsky, *The Permanent Revolution*, Chapter 9. Trotsky, 'Permanent Revolution', http://www.marxists.org/archive/trotsky/works/1931-tpv/rp09.htm.

47 Ibid.

48 J Molyneux, *Leon Trotsky's Theory of Revolution* (London: Macmillan, 1982), p.40. The reference is to G Lukács, *Lenin: a Study on the Unity of his Thought* (London: New Left Books, 1972).

49 Cliff, *Trotsky 1879–1917*, p.65.

50 Trotsky, *My Life*, p.200.

51 L Trotsky, *My Flight From Siberia* (Colombo: Young Socialist Publication, 1969).

52 Trotsky, *My Life*, pp.19–20.

53 L Trotsky, *The War Correspondence of Leon Trotsky: The Balkan Years 1912–1913* (New York: Pathfinder Press, 1991).

54 L Trotsky, 'Political Profiles: Victor and Friedrich Adler' (1922), http://www.marxists.org/archive/trotsky/works/1940/profiles/victor-friedalder.htm.

55 Ibid.

56 Trotsky, *My Life*, p.253.

57 Lunacharsky, *Revolutionary Silhouettes*, p.65.

58 Ibid.

59 I D Thatcher, *Leon Trotsky and World War One: August 1914–February 1917* (New York: St Martin's, 2000).

60 Deutscher, *The Prophet Armed*, p.239.

61 'The Historical Significance of the Russian Revolution', *Socialist History* 22 (2002), pp.56–83, 60.

62 T Ali and P Evans, *Trotsky for Beginners* (London: Writers and Readers, 1980), p.63.

63 J Reed, *Ten Days that Shook the World* (London: Martin Lawrence, 1920), p.10.

64 Lunacharsky, *Revolutionary Silhouettes*, p.65.

65 Trotsky, *My Life*, p.307.

66 L Trotsky, 'For A Workers' United Front Against Fascism', written in exile in Turkey, 8 December 1931, published in *Bulletin of the Opposition*, 27 March 1932.

67 'Letter to the Central Committee, the Moscow and Petrograd Committees and the Bolshevik Members of the Petrograd and Moscow Soviets', in V I Lenin, *Collected Works: Volume 26* (London: Lawrence and Wishart, 1960), pp.87–136.

68   Trotsky, *My Life*, pp.337.

69   Ibid., pp.337–8.

70   Reed, *Ten Days*, p.60.

71   Deutscher, *The Prophet Armed*, p.314.

72   Reed, *Ten Days*, p.109.

73   Cited in Serge, 'Un portrait de Lénine par Trotsky', pp.255–8.

74   S A Smith, *Red Petrograd: Revolution in the Factories 1917–1918* (Cambridge: Cambridge University Press, 1983), p.258.

75   V Serge, *Year One of the Russian Revolution* (London and New York: Bookmarks, Pluto and Writers and Readers, 1992), p.79.

76   D Hallas, *The Comintern* (London: Bookmarks, 1985), p.7.

77   Cited in Serge, '*Un portrait de Lénine par Trotsky*', pp.255–8.

78   Ali and Evans, *Trotsky for Beginner*s, p.80.

79   T Cliff, *Trotsky 1917–1923: The Sword of the Revolution* (London: Bookmarks, 1990), p.33.

80   Deutscher, *The Prophet Armed*, p.444.

81   Ibid.

82   Cliff, *Trotsky 1917-1923*, pp.63, 93–4.

83   Trotsky, *My Life*, p.445.

84   Deutscher, *The Prophet Armed*, p.446.

85   Trotsky, *My Life*, p.20.

86   L Bryant, 'Leon Trotsky: Soviet War Lord', http://www.marxists.org/archive/bryant/works/1923mom/ trotsky.htm.

87   Ibid.

88   Ibid.

89   L Trotsky, *Terrorism and Communism* (London: New Park, 1975), pp.68, 151.

90   'Militarized labour,' writes Tony Cliff, 'is tyrannical and incompatible with working-class self-emancipation, in other words with socialism. Socialism would not only lighten compulsion in the labour field, but would transform its nature, and lead ultimately to its complete abolition.' Cliff, *Trotsky 1917-1923*.

91   Deutscher, *The Prophet Unarmed*, p.509; Cliff, *Trotsky 1917-1923*, pp.168–70.

92   Cliff, *Trotsky 1917-1923*, 168-70

93   Deutscher, *The Prophet Unarmed*, p.509.

94   Ibid.

95   Lunacharsky, *Revolutionary Silhouettes*, p.65.

96 L Trotsky, *Problems of Life* (London: Methuen, 1924); cited in I Deutscher (ed), *The Age of Permanent Revolution: A Trotsky Anthology* (New York: Dell, 1964), p.301.

97 V Serge, *Memoirs of a Revolutionary* 1901–1941, trans and ed P Sedgwick (Oxford and New York: Oxford University Press, 1963), p.128; Serge's shifting views on Kronstadt constitute a major theme in D Cotterill (ed), *The Serge Trotsky Papers: Correspondence and Other Writings between Victor Serge and Leon Trotsky* (London: Pluto Press, 1994).

98 Using the same formula, we could say that the Mensheviks had their chance following February 1917, while Stalin incarnated the very worst habits of Russian populism.

99 The author who has done most to defend the politics of the NEP period is Stephen Cohen. See his *Rethinking the Soviet Experience* (Oxford: Clarendon Press, 1985).

100 L Trotsky, *Literature and Revolution* (London: Redwords, 1991).

101 Deutscher, *The Prophet Unarmed*, p.165.

102 It was an order preventing all permanent organizations of minorities. Even at this late stage, inner-party debate and division were still tolerated.

103 Deutscher, *The Prophet Unarmed*, p.109.

104 W Taubman, *Khrushchev: The Man and His Era* (London: Free Press, 2003), pp.106–7.

105 M Lewin, *Lenin's Last Struggle* (London: Faber and Faber, 1969).

106 Deutscher, *The Prophet Unarmed*, p.16.

107 J Molyneux, *Marxism and the Party* (London: Pluto Press, 1978), p.120.

108 Deutscher, *The Prophet Unarmed*, p.16.

109 L Trotsky, 'For Quality – For Culture!', *Revolutionary History* 7/2 (1999), pp.105–36, 131.

110 Hallas, *The Comintern*, p.7.

111 Ali and Evans, *Trotsky for Beginners*, p.120.

112 Serge, *Memoirs of a Revolutionary*, p.220.

113 L Trotsky, 'The Russian Opposition: Questions and Answers', *The New International*, New York, May 1938. Text available online at http://www.marxists.org/archive/trotsky/works/1927/1927-opposition.htm.

114 Ibid.

115 Ibid.

116 Robert Harvey, *Comrades: The Rise and Fall of World Communism* (London: John Murray, 2003), p.65.

117 Hallas, *The Comintern*, p.7.

118 Deutscher, *The Prophet Unarmed*, pp.392–4.

119 Trotsky, *History of the Russian Revolutiony*, pp.28–38.

120 Ibid.,122-3

121 L Trotsky, *On Lenin: Notes Towards a Biography* (London: Harrap, 1971).

122 Trotsky, *History of the Russian Revolution*, p.17.

123 Deutscher, *The Prophet Outcast: Trotsky 1929–1940* (Oxford: Oxford University Press, 1963), p.220.

124 'The Eighteenth Brumaire of Louis Bonaparte', *Karl Marx and Fredrich Engels, Collected Works: Volume 11* (London: Lawrence and Wishart, 1967), pp.99–197.

125 E Wilson, *To the Finland Station: A Study in the Writing and Acting of History* (London: Penguin, 1992), p.191.

126 Lunacharsky, *Revolutionary Silhouettes*, p.65.

127 Translated from 'Discours prononcé à l'exécutif, le 26 Février 1922, sur le FU', in L Trotsky, *Le mouvement communiste en France 1919–1939* (Paris: Éditions de Minuit, 1977), pp.147–62.

128 L Trotsky, *The Struggle against Fascism in Germany* (New York: Pathfinder Press, 1971), p.136.

129 Ibid.

130 Ali and Evans, *Trotsky for Beginners*, p.145.

131 Trotsky, 'For A Workers' United Front Against Fascism'.

132 Ibid.

133 Ibid.

134 Trotsky, *Struggle against Fascism*, p.144; L Trotsky, *Fascism, Stalinism and the United Front* (London: Bookmarks, 1989).

135 Deutscher, *The Prophet Outcast*, p.197

136 N Geras, 'Marxists before the Holocaust', *New Left Review* 224 (1997), pp.19–38, 19, 26–7.

137 L Trotsky, *The Revolution Betrayed: What is the Soviet Union and Where Is It Going?* (New York: Pathfinder Press, 1972), pp.90, 93, 105, 248, 252–4.

138 Ibid.

139 Ibid.

140 Ibid.

141 Ibid.

142 Cited in Trotsky, *Terrorism and Communism*, pp.51.

143 Ibid., p.188

144 Reproduced at
http://www.marxists.org/archive/trotsky/works/1937/1937-sta.htm.

145 Cited in Deutscher, *The Prophet Outcast*, pp.456

146 Ibid.

147 This is the argument of T Cliff, *State Capitalism in Russia* (London: Pluto Press, 1955), as well as texts by C L R James, Raya Dunayevskaya and others. There were also those who argued that Russia was a 'bureaucratic collectivist' society. Although the analytical roots of this argument were different, its *practical* critique of Trotsky's position (including the idea that Stalinist Russia could not be reformed) was largely the same.

148 Pomper (ed), *Trotsky's Notebooks 1933–1935,* p.83.

149 Trotsky, *The Young Lenin*; Trotsky, *On Lenin*.

150 L Trotsky, *Their Morals and Ours* (New York: Pathfinder Press, 1992).

151 D Cotterill (ed), *The Serge Trotsky Papers*.

152 L Trotsky, *Leon Trotsky on France* (New York: Pathfinder Press, 1979).

153 'The Reply of "the Nucleus" to Trotsky's Two Requests', in A Rosmer (et al), *Trotsky and the Origins of Trotskyism* (London: Francis Boutle, 2002), pp.120–31.

153 D Hallas, 'Trotskyism Reassessed', *International Socialism*, July 1977.

155 Molyneux, *Marxism and the Party*, pp.128–30, 133.

156 Ali and Evans, *Trotsky for Beginners*, p.157.

157 Cohen, *Rethinking the Soviet Experience*.

158 C Porter, *Alexandra Kollontai: A Biography* (London: Virago, 1980), p.344.

159 D Hallas, *Trotsky's Marxism* (London: Pluto Press, 1979), p.98.

160 N S Trotsky, 'How It Happened', *Fourth International*, May 1941.

161 Trotsky, *My Life*, p.xiii-iv.

162 Trotsky, *My Life*, p.xv.

163 Trotsky, *My Life*, p.xxiv.

164 Trotsky, *My Life*, p.xxxiii.

165 L Trotsky, 'Stalin Seeks My Death', in *Writings of Leon Trotsky (1939–40)* (New York: Pathfinder Press, 1973), p.233.

166 N Mosely, *The Assassination of Trotsky* (London: Abacus, 1972), pp.141-5.

167 Ibid.

168 Ibid.

169 Ibid.

170 Cited in Volkogonov, *Trotsky: The Eternal Revolutionary*, p.466

171 Trotsky, 'How it Happened'.

172 Deutscher, *The Prophet Outcast*, pp.477-80.

Disclaimer

The publisher has used its best endeavours to ensure that the URLs for external websites referred to in this book are correct and active at the time of going to press. However, the publisher has no responsibility for the websites and can make no guarantee that a site may remain live or that the content is or will remain appropriate.

Chronology

Year	Age	Life
1879		Trotsky born Lev Davidovich Bronstein at Yanokva, Southern Ukraine.
1881	3	Assassination of Tsar Alexander II by Narodniks.
1883	5	Plekhanov, Zasulich and Axelrod found the Emancipation of Labour group, the first Marxist formation in Russia.
1897	18	Trotsky and friends establish a South Russian Workers' Union.
1898	19	Trotsky imprisoned and jailed.
1900	21	Russian Social Democratic Labour Party (RSDLP) founded. Trotsky sentenced to four years in Siberia. Marries Alexandra Sokolovskaya.

Year	History	Culture
1879	Albert Einstein born.	Anton Bruckner, Sixth Symphony. Tchaikovsky, *Eugene Onegin*. Ibsen, *The Doll's House*. August Strindberg, *The Red Room*.
1881	In Japan, political parties established. Tunisia becomes French protectorate. In Algeria, revolt against the French. In Sudan, Mahdi Holy War (until 1898). In eastern Europe, Jewish pogroms.	Jacques Offenbach, *The Tales of Hoffmann*. Anatole France, *Le Crime de Sylvestre* Bonnard. Henry James, *Portrait of Lady*. Ibsen, *Ghosts*.
1883	Jewish immigration to Palestine (Rothschild Colonies). Germany acquires southwest Africa. In Chicago, world's first sky scraper built.	Antonín Dvorák, *Stabat Mater*. Robert Louis Stevenson, *Treasure Island*.
1897	In Britain, Queen Victoria's Diamond Jubilee. Britain destroys Benin City. Klondike gold rush (until 1899). J J Thomson discovers electron.	Joseph Conrad, *The Nigger of the Narcissus*. Stefan George, *Das Jahr der Seele.* Strindberg, *Inferno*. Edmond Rostand, *Cyrano de Bergerac*.
1898	Spanish-American War: Spain loses Cuba, Puerto Rico and the Philippines. Britain conquers Sudan.	Hector Berlioz, *The Taking of Troy*. Edward Elgar, *Enigma Variations*. George, *Der Teppich des Lebens*.
1900	First Pan-African Conference. In France, Dreyfus pardoned. Relief of Mafeking. In China, Boxer Rebellion (until 1901). Aspirin introduced. First Zeppelin flight.	

Year	Age	Life
1902	23	Publication of Lenin's *What Is to Be Done?* Trotsky's first escape from Siberia.
1903	24	RSDLP split between Bolsheviks and Mensheviks.
1904	25	Trotsky's first resignation from Menshevik fraction.
1905	26	Massacre of peaceful demonstration sparks year of revolution. Trotsky elected to Chair of the St Petersburg Soviet. Trotsky arrested in December as the Revolution collapses.
1906	27	'Results and Prospects' written.
1907	28	Trotsky's second escape from Siberia.
1908	29	Stuttgart conference of the Second International passes a motion for a general strike in the event of war.
1914	35	Start of First World War. Trotsky works for anti-war press.
1915	36	Zimmerwald conference opposes war.

Year	History	Culture
1902	Peace of Vereeniging ends Boer War. Anglo-Japanese alliance.	Debussy, *Pelléas et Mélisande*. Scott Joplin, *The Entertainer*. Hillaire Belloc.
1903	Bolshevik-Menshevik split in Communist Party of Russia. In Russia, pogroms against Jews. In Britain, suffragette movement begins. Panama Canal Zone granted to US to build and manage water way. Wright Brothers' first flight.	Henry James, *The Ambassadors*.
1904	France and Britain sign Entente Cordiale. Russo-Japanese War. Photoelectric cell invented.	Puccini, *Madama Butterfly*. G K Chesterton, *The Napoleon of Notting Hill*. Jack London, *The Sea Wolf*. J M Barrie, *Peter Pan*. Chekhov, The Cherry Orchard.
1905	Korea becomes protectorate of Japan.	Richard Strauss, *Salome*. Albert Einstein, *Special Theory of Relativity*. Paul Cézanne, *Les Grandes Baigneuses*.
1906	Algeciras Conference resolves dispute between France and Germany over Morocco. Duma created in Russia. Revolution in Iran.	Henri Matisse, *Bonheur de vivre*. Maxim Gorky, *The Mother* (until 1907).
1907	Anglo-Russian Entente. Electric washing-machine invented.	Conrad, *The Secret Agent*. Rainer Maria Rilke, *Neue Gedichte*.
1908	Bulgaria becomes independent. Austria-Hungary annexes Bosnia-Herzegovina.	Gustav Mahler, *Das Lied von der Erde* (until 1909). E M Forster, *A Room with a View*. Cubism begins with Picasso and Braque.
1914	28 June: Archduke Franz Ferdinand assassinated in Sarajevo. First World War begins. Panama Canal opens. Egypt becomes British protectorate.	James Joyce, *The Dubliners*.Ezra Pound, *Des Imagistes*.
1915	Dardanelles/Gallipoli campaign (until 1916). Italy denounces its Triple Alliance with Germany and Austria-Hungary.	John Buchan, *The Thirty-Nine Steps*. D H Lawrence, *The Rainbow*. Ezra Pound, *Cathay*. Marcel Duchamp, *The Large Glass* or *The Bride Stripped Bare by her Bachelors,Even* (until 1923).

Year	Age	Life
1915	36	Trotsky works to reconcile Mensheviks and Bolshevics in Paris.
1916	37	Trotsky expelled from France; arrives in the United States via Spain.
1917	38	February Revolution. Trotsky and Lenin return to Russia. Both demand a second revolution. Trotsky joins Bolsheviks. 'July Days', premature attempt to topple Provisional Government. General Kornilov's attempted coup against Kerensky. Trotsky again elected chair of the Petrograd Soviet and helps plan October insurrection. Later becomes Commissar for Foreign Affairs. Trotsky at Brest-Litovsk to negotiate peace with Germany.
1918	39	Peace signed: Soviet Union loses Finland and Ukraine. Civil war begins. Trotsky becomes Commissar for War and tours the front line by train. Writes *Terrorism and Communism*. Revolution in Germany.
1919	40	Defeat of second Spartacist uprising in Berlin.
1920	41	Trotsky calls for labour organizations to be subordinated to the state.
1921	42	Kronstadt rebellion. Announcement of New Economic Policy. Ban on permanent factions within Communist Party.

Year	History	Culture
1915	In Britain, Herbert Asquith forms coalition government. In Brussels, Germans execute Edith Cavell. In Britain, Women's Institute founded. Albert Einstein introduces general theory of relativity.	Pablo Picasso, *Harlequin*.
1916	Battle of Somme. Battle of Jutland. Easter Rising in Ireland. Arabs revolt against Ottoman Turks.	Guillaume Apollinaire, *Le poète assassiné*. G B Shaw, *Pygmalion*. Dada movement launched in Zurich with Cabaret Voltaire.
1917	In Russia, revolutions in February and October. Tsar Nicholas II abdicates. Communists seize power under Vladimir Lenin. Battle of Passchendaele. US enters first world war	First recording of New Orleans jazz. Franz Kafka, *Metamorphosis*. T S Eliot, *Prufrock and Other Observations*. Giurgio de Chirico, *Le Grand Métaphysiqu*
1918	Treaty of Brest-Litovsk between Russia and the Central Powers. In Russia, Tsar Nicholas II and family executed. 11 November: Armistice agreement ends First World War. British take Palestine and Syria. In UK, women over 30 get right to vote.	Oswald Spengler, *The Decline of the West*, Volume 1. Amédée Ozenfant and Le Corbusier, Après le Cubisme. Paul Klee, Gartenplan. Tarzan of the Apes with Elmo Lincoln
1919	Treaty of Versailles. Spartacist revolt in Germany. Poland, Hungary, Czechoslovakia, Estonia, Lithuania and Latvia become republics. Comintern held in Moscow. In US, prohibition begins. Irish Civil War (until 1921).	Franz Kafka, *In the Penal Colony*. J M Keynes, *The Economic Consequences of the Peace*. The Bauhaus founded in Weimar. United Artists formed with Charlie Chaplin, Mary Pickford, Douglas Fairbanks and D W Grifith as partners.
1920	IRA formed. First meeting of League of Nations.	Edith Wharton, *The Age of Innocence*.
1921	National Economic Policy in Soviet Union.	Sergey Prokofiev, *The Love of Three Oranges*. Luigi Pirandello, *Six Characters in Search of*

Year	Age	Life
1922	43	Stalin becomes General Secretary of the Communist Party.
1923	44	Lenin's Testament urges removal of Stalin. Further hoped-for revolution in Germany fails.
1924	45	Death of Lenin. Trotsky's *The Lessons of October* published.
1925	46	Trotsky removed as Commissar for War.
1926	47	Failure of the General Strike in Britain.
1927	48	Defeat of Chinese working-class uprising. Trotsky now joined by Zinoviev and Kamenev in United Opposition.
1928	49	Trotsky sent to Alma Ata.
1929	50	Stalin defeats Bukharin. Trotsky exiled to Prinkipo Island, Turkey. *Bulletin of the Opposition* appears. Wall Street Crash.
1930	51	Trotsky warns of threat posed by Hitler.
1933	54	Hitler comes to power in Germany.

Year	History	Culture
1922	Soviet Union formed. Benito Mussolini's fascists march on Rome.	*an Author*. Chaplin, *The Kid*. T S Eliot, *The Waste Land*. Joyce, *Ulysses*.
1923	Ottoman empire ends; Palestine, Transjordan and Iraq to Britain; Syria to France.	Le Corbusier, *Vers une architecture*.
1924	Kafka dies.	Forster, *A Passage to India*.Kafka, *The Hunger Artist*. Thomas Mann, *The Magic Mountain*. André Breton, first surrealist manifesto.
1925	Pact of Locarno. Chiang Kai-shek launches campaign to unify China. Discovery of ionosphere.	Erik Satie dies. F Scott Fitzgerald, *The Great Gatsby*. Kafka, *The Trial*. Adolf Hitler, *Mein Kempf* (Vol. 1).Sergey Eisenstein, Battleship Potemkin. Television invented.
1926	Germany joins League of Nations.	Puccini, *Turandot*. Kafka, *The Castle*.
1927	Charles Lindbergh flies across Atlantic.	Martin Heidegger, *Being and Time*. Virginia Woolf, *To the Lighthouse*.
1928	Kellogg-Briand Pact for Peace. Alexander Fleming discovers penicillin.	BBC public radio launched. Maurice Ravel, *Boléro*. Kurt Weill, The Threepenny Opera. Huxley, *Point Counter Point*.D H Lawrence, *Lady Chatterley's Lover*. W B Yeats, *The Tower*. Walt Disney, *Steamboat Willie*.
1929	Lateran Treaty. Yugoslavia under kings of Serbia. Wall Street crash.Young Plan for Germany.	William Faulkner, *The Sound and the Fury*. Robert Graves, *Good-bye to All That*. Ernest Hemingway, *A Farewell to Arms*. Erich Remarque, *All Quiet on the Western Front*. Jean Cocteau, *Les Enfants Terribles*.
1930	London Round-Table Conferences on India. Mahatma Gandhi leads Salt March in India. Frank Whittle patents turbo-jet engine. Pluto discovered.	W H Auden, *Poems*. T S Eliot, 'Ash Wednesday'. William Faulkner, *As I lay Dying*. Evelyn Waugh, *Vile Bodies*.
1933	Nazi Party wins German elections. Adolf Hitler appointed	André Malraux, *La condition humaine*. Gertrude Stein, *The Autobiography of*

Year	Age	Life
1933	54	Zina, Trotsky's daughter dies.
1934	55	Purges in Soviet Union.
1935	56	Trotsky moves to Norway. *The Revolution Betrayed* published.
1936	57	Spanish Civil War. Trotsky arrives in Mexico.
1938	59	Leon Sedov, Trotsky's son, murdered in Paris.
1940	61	Trotsky assassinated.

Year	History	Culture
1933	chancellor. Hitler forms Third Reich. F D Roosevelt president in US; launches New Deal.	*Alice B Toklas*.
1934	In Germany, the Night of the Long Knives. In China, the Long March. Enrico Fermi sets off first controlled nuclear reaction.	Dmitri Shostakovich, *The Lady Macbeth of Mtsensk*. Agatha Christie, *Murder on the Orient Express*. Fitzgerald, *Tender is the Night*.Henry Miller, *Tropic of Cancer*.
1935	In Germany, Nuremberg Laws enacted. Philippines becomes self-governing. Italy invades Ethiopia.	George Gershwin, *Porgy and Bess*. Richard Strauss, *Die Schweigsam Frau*. Christopher Isherwood, *Mr Norris Changes Trains*. Marx Brothers, *A Night at the Opera*.
1936	Germany occupies Rhineland. Edward VIII abdicates throne in Britain; George VI becomes king. Léon Blum forms "Popular Front" government in France. Anti-Comintern Pact between Japan and Germany. Spanish Civil War (until 1939).	Prokofiev, *Peter and the Wolf*. A J Ayer, *Language, Truth and Logic*. BBC public television founded.
1938	In Soviet Union, trial of Nikolai Bukharin and other political leaders. Kristallnacht: in Germany, Jewish houses, synagogues and schools are burnt down, and shops looted. Austrian Anschluss with Germany. Munich Crisis. Czechoslovakia cedes Sudetenland. In England, IRA bombings. In east and west Africa, Pan-Africanist movement gains strength. Otto Hahn and F Strassman discover nuclear fission.	Elizabeth Bowen, *The Death of the Heart*. Graham Greene, *Brighton Rock*. Evelyn Waugh, *Scoop*. Sergey Eisenstein, *Alexander Nevsky*.
1940	Germany occupies France, Belgium, the Netherlands, Norway and Denmark.	Graham Greene, *The Power and the Glory*. Ernest Hemingway, *For Whom the Bell Tolls*. Chaplin, *The Great Dictator*.

Further Reading

Unlike Marx, Engels and Lenin, there is no edition of Trotsky's collected works available in English translation. A Russian edition of Trotsky's *Collected Works* was in preparation in the mid-1920s, but it was prevented by Stalin in 1927 and much of Trotsky's early writing remains unavailable.

Various selected works have been published, however, including *The Age of Permanent Revolution: A Trotsky Anthology* (New York: Dell, 1964). There is also a 14-volume *Writings of Leon Trotsky* (New York: Pathfinder Press, 1975–9), but this covers only the years 1929–40.

Trotsky's major works are published separately. His greatest book is almost certainly *The History of the Russian Revolution*, but at more than a thousand pages it is a daunting place to start. His memoir *My Life* was the most important source for this biography and at 600 pages is a slightly lighter introduction. Of the secondary sources, Isaac Deutscher's biography is a brilliant, literary account. Ian Thatcher's is the most recent, while Tony Cliff gives an activist's perspective.

Works by Leon Trotsky

1905 (1907; London: Penguin, 1974).

The Challenge of the Left Opposition (New York: Pathfinder Press, 1975).

In Defense of Marxism (New York: Pathfinder Press, 1973).

Europe and America: Two Speeches on Imperialism (New York: Pathfinder Press, 1971).

Fascism, Stalinism and the United Front (London: Bookmarks, 1989).

Fascism: What It Is and How to Fight It (1944; New York: Pathfinder Press, 1969).

The First Five Years of the Communist International (1927; London: New Park, 1973, 2 volumes).

Flight From Siberia (1907; Colombo: Young Socialist Publications, 1969).

The History of the Russian Revolution (1932; London: Pluto Press, 1985).

Leon Trotsky Speaks (New York: Pathfinder Press, 1972).

Literature and Revolution (1924; London: Redwords, 1991).

Marxism and Terrorism (New York: Pathfinder Press, 1974).

Military Writings (1918–19; New York: Pathfinder Press, 1969).

My Life: An Attempt at an Autobiography (1930; London: Penguin, 1975).

On France (New York: Pathfinder Press, 1979).

On Lenin: Notes Towards a Biography (1924; London: Harrap, 1971).

On the Jewish Question (New York: Pathfinder Press, 1970).

The Permanent Revolution (New York: Pathfinder Press, 1969).

Problems of the Chinese Revolution (1927; Ann Arbor: University of Michigan Press, 1967).

Problems of Everyday Life (London: Methuen, 1924).

Results and Prospects (1906; New York: Pathfinder Press, 1978).

The Revolution Betrayed: What Is the Soviet Union and Where Is It Going? (1937; New York: Pathfinder Press, 1972).

The Spanish Revolution 1931–39 (New York: Pathfinder Press, 1972).

The Struggle against Fascism in Germany (New York: Pathfinder Press, 1971).

Stalin (1945; New York: Stein and Day, 1970).

The Stalin School of Falsification (1937; New York: Pathfinder Press, 1972).

Terrorism and Communism (1920; London: New Park, 1975).

Their Morals and Ours (1938; New York: Pathfinder Press, 1992).

Third International after Lenin (1928; New York: Pathfinder Press, 1971)

The Transitional Program for Socialist Revolution (1938; Pathfinder Press, 1971).

Trotsky's Diary in Exile (New York: Atheneum Publishers, 1964).

Trotsky's Notebooks 1933–1935: Writings on Lenin, Dialectics and Evolutionism (New York: Columbia University Press, 1986).

Trotsky's Writings on Britain (London: New Park, 1974, 3 volumes).

The War Correspondence of Leon Trotsky: The Balkan Years 1912–1913 (New York: Pathfinder Press, 1981).

The Young Lenin (London: Penguin, 1972).

Woman and the Family (New York: Pathfinder Press, 1973).

Biographies

Ali, T and Evans, P, *Trotsky for Beginners* (London: Writers and Readers, 1980).

Broué, P, *Trotsky* (Paris: Fayard, 1988).

Cliff, T, *Trotsky 1879–1917: Towards October* (London: Bookmarks, 1989).

———, *Trotsky 1917–1923: The Sword of the Revolution* (London: Bookmarks, 1990).

———, *Trotsky 1923–1927: Fighting the Rising Stalinist Bureaucracy* (London: Bookmarks, 1991).

———, *Trotsky 1927–1940: The Darker the Night the Brighter the Star* (London: Bookmarks, 1993).

Deutscher, I, *The Prophet Armed: Trotsky 1871–1929* (London: Oxford university Press 1954).

———, *The Prophet Unarmed: Trotsky 1921–1929* (London: Oxford University Press 1959).

———, *The Prophet Outcast: Trotsky 1929–1940* (Oxford: OUP, 1963).

Eastman, M, *Leon Trotsky: The Portrait of a Youth* (London: Faber and Faber, 1926).

Hallas, D, *Trotsky's Marxism* (London: Pluto, 1979).

Howe, I, *Trotsky* (London: Fontana, 1978).

Molyneux, J, *Leon Trotsky's Theory of Revolution* (London: Macmillan, 1982).

Thatcher, I D, *Leon Trotsky and World War One: August 1914–February 1917* (New York: St Martin's, 2000).

———, *Trotsky* (London: Routledge, 2003).

Volkogonov, D, *Trotsky: The Eternal Revolutionary* (London: Harper Collins, 1994).

Other Secondary Literature

Cohen, S, *Rethinking the Soviet Experience* (Oxford: Clarendon, 1985).

Draper, H, *The Two Souls of Socialism* (London: Bookmarks, 1997).

Flett, K and Renton, D, *New Approaches to Socialist History* (Bristol: New Clarion, 2003).

Haynes, M, *Russia: Class and Power 1917–2000* (London: Bookmarks, 2002).

Kowalski, R, *The Russian Revolution 1917–1921* (London: Routledge, 1997).

Lunacharsky, A, *Revolutionary Silhouettes* (London: Penguin, 1967).

Luxemburg, R, *The Accumulation of Capital* (London: Routledge and Kegan Paul, 2003).

Molyneux, J, *Marxism and the Party* (London: Pluto Press, 1978).

Perry, M, *Marxism and History* (London: Palgrave, 2002).

Renton, D, *Classical Marxism* (Bristol: New Clarion, 2002).

——, *Dissident Marxism* (London: Zed, 2003)

Rosmer, A (et al), *Trotsky and the Origins of Trotskyism* (London: Francis Boutle, 2002).

Serge, V, *Memoirs of a Revolutionary 1901–1941* (Oxford and New York: Oxford University Press , 1963).

——, *Year One of the Russian Revolution* (London and New York: Bookmarks, Pluto and Writers and Readers, 1992).

Smith, S A, *Red Petrograd: Revolution in the factories 1917-1918* (Cambridge: Cambridge University Press, 1983).

Wilson, E, *To the Finland Station: A Study in the Writing and Acting of History* (London: Penguin, 1992).

Picture Sources

The author and the publishers wish to express their thanks to the following sources of illustrative material and/or permission to reproduce it. They will make proper acknowledgements in future editions in the event that any omissions have occurred.

AKG-Images London: pp. 4, 12, 15, 23, 34, 41, 43, 59, 63, 114, 137. Corbis: pp. 20, 83, 98, 118. Mary Evans Picture Library: pp. iii, 136. Novosti: pp. 71, 77, 88, 101, 107, 124, 135, 139. Topham Picturepoint: pp. 51, 54, 65, 69, 80, 96, 128, 138, 142.

Index

LIFE & TIMES FROM HAUS

Churchill
by Sebastian Haffner
'One of the most brilliant things of
any length ever written about
Churchill.' *TLS*
1-904341-07-1 (pb) £8.99
1-904341-06-3 (hb) £12.99

Dietrich
by Malene Skaerved
'It is probably the best book ever on
Marlene.' C. Downes
1-904341-13-6 (pb) £8.99
1-904341-12-8 (hb) £12.99

Beethoven
by Martin Geck
'. . . this little gem is a truly handy
reference.' *Musical Opinion*
1-904341-00-4 (pb) £8.99
1-904341-03-9 (hb) £12.99

Prokofiev
by Thomas Schipperges
'beautifully made, . . . well-produced
photographs, . . . with useful
historical nuggets.' *The Guardian*
1-904341-32-2 (pb) £8.99
1-904341-34-9 (hb) £12.99

Curie
by Sarah Dry
'. . . this book could hardly be bettered'
New Scientist
selected as **Outstanding Academic Title**
by *Choice*
1-904341-29-2 (pb) £8.99

Einstein
by Peter D Smith
'Concise, complete, well-produced and
lively throughout, . . . a bargain at the
price.' *New Scientist*
1-904341-15-2 (pb) £8.99
1-904341-14-4 (hb) £12.99

Casement
by Angus Mitchell
'hot topic' *The Irish Times*
1-904341-41-1 (pb) £8.99

Britten
by David Matthews
'I have read them all – but none with as
much enjoyment as this.' *Literary Review*
1-904341-21-7 (pb) £8.99
1-904341-39-X (hb) £12.99

De Gaulle
by Julian Jackson
'this concise and distinguished book'
Andrew Roberts *Sunday Telegraph*
1-904341-44-6 (pb) £8.99

Orwell
by Scott Lucas
'short but controversial assessment . . .
is sure to raise a few eyebrows' *Sunday
Tasmanian*
1-904341-33-0 (pb) £8.99

Bach
by Martin Geck
'The production values of the book are
exquisite, too.'
The Guardian
1-904341-16-0 (pb) £8.99
1-904341-35-7 (hb) £12.99

Kafka
by Klaus Wagenbach
'One of the most useful books about Kafka
ever published' *Frankfurter Allgemeine
Zeitung*
1-904341-02 -0 (PB) £8.99
1-904341-01-2 (hb) £12.99

Dostoevsky
by Richard Freeborn
'. . . wonderful . . . a learned guide'
The Sunday Times
1-904341-27-6 (pb) £8.99

Brahms
by Hans Neunzig
'readable, comprehensive and
attractively priced'
The Irish Times
1-904341-17-9 (pb) £8.99

Verdi
by Barbara Meier
'These handy volumes fill a gap in the
market . . . admirably.' *Classic fM*
1-904341-21-7 (pb) £8.99
1-904341-39-X (hb) L12.99

Armstrong
by David Bradbury
'generously illustrated . . . a fine and well-
researched introduction' George Melly
Daily Mail
1-904341-46-2 (pb) £8.99
1-904341-47-0 (hb) £12.99